The CHRIST life for YOUR life

by

F. B. MEYER

moody press
chicago

ISBN: 0-8024-1302-1

Printed in the United States of America

Contents

A Castaway	5
"Marred: So He Made It Again"	17
The Natural Man	29
The Substitution of the Christ-Life for the Self-Life	42
Christ the Complement of Our Need	52
Deliverance from the Power of Sin	62
God's Two Men	73
The Anointing with the Holy Spirit	85
The Infilling of the Holy Spirit	98
Heart-Rest	114

THESE ADDRESSES were delivered at the Carnegie Hall, New York, during an ever-memorable week, and in part also, at the Tremont Temple Boston, and in Philadelphia. In answer to many urgent demands they are printed almost as they were delivered, from the reporter's notes: therefore may lack in literary finish—but the truth is the main consideration. And I believe that what is taught here will give a glimpse into those deeper aspects of Christianity, which are best adapted to nourish and quicken the inner life.

F. B. MEYER

A Castaway

I INVITE YOUR ATTENTION to a few words found in I Corinthians 9:27: "Lest that by any means, when I have preached to others, I myself should be a castaway."

Paul was too eager and too practical a man to dally with a bogey dread. Since then he intimates that it was his daily fear lest, after having preached to others, he might himself be a castaway, I suppose that there were but few hours in his life when this dread did not haunt him. After he had founded so many churches, written so many epistles, and exercised so widespread an influence, in his quiet moments he was perpetually face to face with this awful nightmare, that the day might come when he would be a castaway; and the thought drove him almost to madness. When he was traveling over the blue Aegean, when he was sitting making his tents, when he was engaged in dictating his epistles, the thought would come back and back upon his heart, "I may yet be a castaway."

Have you ever feared this? I am not sure that a man ever reaches his highest development without something of the element of fear, and I ask you now if in your life you know something of this haunting dread. May I confess to you that it has become a great dread of my own?

and if many days pass, and no one writes to tell me of help derived from my ministry, and no one comes to join our church, and no one seems to be influenced by my life or word, I sit myself down and say, "Good God, has the time come at last to me when for some reason I, too, am to be a castaway?"

And reverently, humbly, but most searchingly, I ask you, my reader, whether it may not be possible that this very moment you are already a castaway.

"A CASTAWAY" IN WHAT SENSE?

Is it to be supposed for a moment that the Apostle thought that when once the believer has fled to Christ he can be cast out into the outer darkness where there is weeping, and wailing, and gnashing of teeth? Is it possible for a limb to be torn from the mystical body of Christ, for a jewel to be snatched from out of His crown, for a sheep to be devoured from His flock? Are there any unfinished pictures in God's gallery, any incomplete statues in His workshop? Does God begin a work in the soul and leave it incomplete and unperfected? We cannot believe it.

It is said of Rowland Hill, my great predecessor at Christ Church, London, that when an old man of eighty-four and just before he died, one Sunday night when the lights had been put out in Surrey Chapel, the verger in attendance heard him go to and fro in the aisle, singing to himself:

> When I am to die, "Receive me"—I'll cry,
> For Jesus has loved me, I cannot tell why;
> But this I do find, we two are so joined,
> He'll not be in heaven and leave me behind.

If you have faith as a grain of mustard seed, if it is directed toward Christ, a union has been formed between Him and you which neither heaven nor earth nor hell nor time nor eternity can ever break.

And yet the Apostle feared he would be a castaway. What did he mean?

One day I was calling on a brother clergyman. He took me out into his garden to an outhouse, against the side of which was resting one of the old-fashioned bicycles with a very tall wheel. I said to him, "Do you ever ride this?"

Said he, "No; see how rusty it is. I have not been on it for many months. I have got something better, something that suits my purpose better," pointing to another and a newer bicycle on the other side of the house.

I said to myself, "Then this is a castaway."

When stylographic pens first came out, I purchased one in the hope that it would serve me perfectly. But I was sadly disappointed. Sometimes when I attempted to use it, it was unwilling to serve me. At other times it was profuse in inking the finger. Finally I discarded it in hopelessness and purchased another pen. The one I now hold serves me perfectly, and I have no difficulty whatever in performng by its means any writing upon which I have set my heart. But I keep the other one. It lies in the drawer of my bureau, and often when I am putting my things together to go upon some journey, I think I hear it saying to itself as it lies there, "Ah, he is going away without me again! There was a time when he never left home without taking me with him; he never wrote a letter without me; he never composed an article but that

I first knew its contents; but for these many days and months I have been lying here unused."

That disused stylographic pen is my conception of what Paul meant when he said he feared being a castaway.

You must know that this man loved to save men. It was the passion of his life. Send him to Philippi, and he will not be there a week before he has won his first European convert, Lydia. Let him be bound in jail, and before midnight he will have baptized his jailer. Send him to Athens, and though he is all alone, he will gather a congregation upon Mars' Hill within a week or two. Put him alongside of Aquila and Priscilla at the bench, and he will make tents and talk to them in such good wise that they will become Christians. Stand him before his judge, and the latter will cry, "Almost thou persuadest me to be a Christian!" Let him go to Rome, tied to a Roman sentry, and he will speak to these men, one after another, in such fashion that the whole Pretorian camp will be infused with the love of God. His passion was to save men. I do not believe that if he were alive to-day, he would be in a streetcar, or a railway car, or on board a steamer without buttonholing some man and speaking to him about his soul and his Saviour. The whole passion of the man was to save some; but he feared that unless he took good care, the hour might come in his life when Christ would say, "Thou hast served me well, but thou shalt serve me no more. Of late thou hast become indolent, and choked with pride, and I have not secured thy whole obedience. I am now compelled to call upon some soul more alert, more obedient than thee;

and that man I will use to do the work that thou mightest have done, but which thou didst fail to accomplish."

This comes home upon us, brother ministers. I am speaking to some who in their earlier life were wondrously used of God in soul-winning, as they went from the seminary or the college, and took their first church. Sunday after Sunday the inquiry-room was crowded. The simple villagers, from their lips, heard the Word of God, and were converted, and the communicant's roll was weekly increased. The boys of the neighborhood were attracted, and won like jewels for Christ. Am I not speaking to women who in their first burst of love to Christ wore the signs of holy earnestness in their circles of society, so that all who came in contact with them were made to feel the power of a genuine love to God? May we not all look back to days upon days, long passed, when we were the channels through which Jesus spoke and wrought, and the Holy Ghost was poured upon men? But what has happened? We preach the same old sermons, but Christ is apparently indifferent to them. We go through the same mechanical routine, but there is no stir of life. These many days have passed, and there have been no additions to our church roll. We have won men to ourselves, but not to Christ. And so it seems as though whilst men flattered us, and whilst we had a certain complacency in their applause, heaven passed on unheeding, the souls of men were unreached, and our churches were just dying of inanition; the old passing on to God, but the young untouched, unsaved.

May not the question therefore come to us now, "Perhaps, after all, Christ has ceased to use me! Christ has no further purpose for me! I am too clumsy, too obtuse, too disobedient, too full of myself, too much out of touch with Him! And so I am to be put on the shelf!" Like those great stones in the quarry at Baalbec—almost completely quarried, but yet the temple was finished without them! May not this question go through the audience, "Am I a castaway? I belong to Christ, and when I die I believe I will go home to Him. I know that He has saved me by His precious blood; but has He ceased to use me?"

Look for a moment upon the pages of Scripture, and see how they are

LITTERED WITH CASTAWAYS!

Let us then understand why men are cast away.

I take the first case, that of Esau. He comes in from hunting. He is born to the birthright. The birthright includes the power of standing between God and the clan, speaking to God for men. He is famished. Yonder is the steaming mess of pottage prepared by his brother Jacob.

"Give me that red lentil pottage," he cries.

Jacob, crafty in heart, bargains, "Give me your spiritual birthright."

Is there not here some Christian, who in the past has had some steaming mess of pottage appealing to the senses? There is not one of us who has not been tempted by some temptation to sense. Aye, it may be there is many a man who is glancing back into his past life, and who knows that he has yielded—not once or twice, but oftener—to the appeal to the senses. He has taken a drink, or indulged some other appetite, and has despised his birthright.

I once heard a story that made my heart ache, of a gray-headed man who had been greatly used of God. In his home he had fallen into one gross act of immorality. Another went to accuse him of his crime. They were sitting together at the tea-table. His portion was not sufficiently sweet; and in the midst of this talk upon which depended whether or not the one should be held guilty, and whether he should be permitted to continue in his ministry, he said slightingly, "My tea is sour. Give me some more sugar."

He cared more at that awful moment of his life whether or not the tea was sour or sweet enough, while his power as a minister of God's holy gospel was trembling in the balance. He did eat and drink, and despised his birthright.

Have *you* never eaten and drunken, and despised your birthright? Are you quite sure that some silent and beautiful form has not come into your life and destroyed your heart's true love? Are you quite sure that there is not in you some hungry appetite that has sought satisfaction?

"Give it me. I must have it. I cannot live without it. Even though I have not quite the spiritual power that I had, give it me."

So men despise their birthright still, and they are cast away. Esau became a prince in this world, and the father of a line of dukes, and all the world flattered him and thought him a prosperous and successful man, but God wrote over him the awful epitaph, "This man is a castaway. He did eat and drink, and rose up, and went his way: thus he despised his birthright."

I turn the page of Scripture, and come to the first king

of Israel, Saul. A noble man in many respects, he was sent by God to fulfill His mission, but he put a reserve upon his obedience, and told Samuel with a kind of pious blarney, "Blessed be thou of the Lord: I have performed the commandment of the Lord."

The old prophet at that moment detected the lowing of the herd and the bleating of the flock, and said very significantly, "Performed the commandment of the Lord! What means then this bleating of the sheep in mine ears and the lowing of the oxen which I hear?"

I am not here to denounce specific forms of sin. If I did, the result would be that the people who were not directly attacked would hold up their umbrellas and let my words drip upon some others whom they think they would fit, and they would suppose therefore that they passed muster. But I am here to bring you face to face with the eternal God, to lead your consciences before the great White Throne, and let the light of the eternal purity of God blaze like a flashlight upon them. It will be for you to determine if under the profession of obedience there are some flocks and herds that you are reserving for yourselves. It is possible when you go to a man's home, or when you even smell his breath, or when you hear him speak, to know whether or not he has given up all for God. Some unfortunate sheep starts bleating. Saul professed obedience, but kept back something for himself; and God rejected him. He lingered ten years more on the throne, but he was a castaway. A young David was already anointed to succeed him.

So when I pass through the Word of God and take case after case, my heart bleeds and cries out because I know not who may be here. I would speak with all tenderness and all pity and all love. I have not come to scathe anyone. I have not come to denounce. It is because I know what the horror of that pit is, and what the horror of being cast away from God's service means, that I now speak in this way. You expected that I would bring you a system of spiritual truth,—and I have such a system to present; you expected that I was going to teach you how to receive the Holy Ghost of Pentecost, so that every day might be a Pentecost—and I have that blessed message to tell you; but I dare not come to those deep and blessed subjects until I have introduced into your heart a spirit of self-scrutiny and searching, that everyone may ask himself, "Can it be that though I am a minister, or an officer of the church, and bear around the holy elements on Sunday at the Communion service, and give my money to philanthropic objects—can it be that in God's sight I am a castaway?"

Coming out of a meeting recently a brother minister came up to me, took me by the hand, shook it warmly, and said, "I have enjoyed your meeting so much."

Directly he said that I knew that I had failed. When a man says that he has enjoyed a meeting like this, I know that I have not touched him.

You remember when Jacob got down into the Jabbok ford, how beneath those Syrian stars he wrestled with the angel, and the angel with him. Presently the angel put forth his hand and touched the sinew of his strength, and he limped. Do you think it is possible that Jacob could have limped into the camp next morning, and going to his beloved Rachel, have said to her, "O Rachel, we have had a lovely time all night. I have enjoyed it!"

Rather he must have said to her, "I have had a night

which has blasted my strength, which has left a scar upon me which I shall carry till I die. O woman, I have fought with the angel of God's love!"

This may be the beginning of

A NEW ERA IN MANY A LIFE.

But we must begin at the bottom; we must begin at the root of our self-confidence. The prime cause of all failure in private life as well as in public ministry is the assertion of self. As long as men and women think it is all right with them, nothing can be done for them. It is only when there is excited within them a fear that after all things may not be quite so well as they seem, a dread that after all they may have made a mistake and be self-deceived, it is only then that in the secret of their own chambers they begin to ask God, "Am I just what I expected?" It is then that the heart is laid open, and they may be brought to understand how a man may be almost a castaway and yet be taken back to the bosom of Christ as Peter was; for within six weeks the man who was nearly cast away became the Apostle of Pentecost.

Paul said, "Lest I should be a castaway. Therefore, though I have a perfect right to go to an idol temple, I shall not go for fear other men seeing me go may follow me, and what might be innocent to me might be death to them. Lest I should ruin any man's soul by going, I will abstain. I have a perfect right, if I choose, to take a wife; but I shall not do it. I will live a bachelor life, and toil with my hands, because by being lonesome myself I may touch some other man who is lonesome too, and by working with my own hands I shall stay upon the bench beside others who will be drawn to me by sympathy.

There are many things which this body of mine may have in innocence, but I shall not take them because I wish to keep my body under, lest it should master me and cause me to be a castaway."

Christ waits—the sweet strong, pure Son of God—His heart yearning over men and yearning to pour itself through us to save them. But many of us have choked Him, resisted Him, thwarted Him. One feels like asking the whole audience to fall before Him in confession, and to ask that this holy day may not pass until He has restored us to fellowship with Himself.

My friend, Dr. Harry Grattan Guinness, told me once that all the water supply had become choked out of their college in Derbyshire, England. They could not obtain one drop of water from the bottom to the top of the house. They searched the cisterns, and inspected the taps and the whole machinery, and found no cause. At last they went to the junction between the main reservoir-pipe and their house-pipe, and there in the orifice, in the joint between the two, squatted a huge toad, which (as they were told) had probably come in as a tadpole, had fed upon the water, and had grown to this size, so that the whole water was stopped because it choked the orifice.

Your life has been dry lately; no tear, no prayer, no fervor. You have not met Christ, you have not seen His face for many a long day, He has not used you. It must be because there is something in your heart, innocent once but injurious now. May God show you what it is! Get quiet, and prostrate yourself before God. If people want to speak to you brush past them. If they want to detain you with small talk, leave them. Cast yourself down in some solitary place before God, and say, "May God forgive me! May God show me the sin, show me what it is that hinders me, show me what has nearly wrecked my life. Whatever comes, may I not be a castaway, but still used by Thee through the Holy Ghost for Christ."

"Marred: So He Made It Again"

ONCE PAGANNINI, standing before a great audience, broke string after string in his violin, until only one was left. He held up his violin, and said, "One string and Pagannini."

Now we want one man and God; God working through a man so that the man is the channel. But before God can work by a man, he must be right, and I have to speak now on how God can make a man right, fit for service.

In the preceding address we came to despair. We stood upon the brink of the precipice and looked down into the dark, fearing that we might be castaways. Now I take for my text the words:

"He made it again." Jeremiah 18:4.

What did he make again? Jeremiah was a disappointed man. He thought he could do no more to stay the people from destruction. His heart was breaking. God told him to go down to the potter's house, and there he saw the potter take a piece of clay and place it on a wheel. As he stood there to watch, the potter shaped it: it rose beneath his hand into a fair and lovely shape. But just as it was complete, and it seemed as though nothing more was needed, it crumbled beneath his hand. Some part of it fell upon the wheel, some part upon the ground. Jeremiah thought that the potter would take another piece of clay and make that clay fulfill his plan, but instead he stooped and gathered the broken clay with his hand, picked it from the ground, and kneading it with his hand he placed it once more upon the wheel and began to make that clay again; and presently a vessel as fair as possible stood complete, ready to be taken to the kiln to be baked and made permanent.

Away back in your life God took you and placed you upon the wheel, and for these many years God has sought to make you fair. But I know not why, I cannot tell—God knows—you know—there has come a flaw and break, and you are a piece of broken pottery. Your life is a marred life, your ideal a broken ideal, and all around there lie the littered pieces of the man or the woman that you might have been.

But now what shall you do? God put you in that place for a high purpose, but you have missed your mark. Shall God take another man and give him your wealth, another woman and give her your position? Shall God take another student and put him in your church? Shall God call another body to perform the work your church should do? Not yet, not yet. He might take another piece of clay and make that a vessel, but instead He comes again to seek you. His hand is passing through this audience to find you, that the broken pieces of your life, your marred and spoiled ideal, may be made over again. Clergyman, merchant, lady of fashion, Christian worker, student, singer,—God's hand is feeling for you now. The hand of God is, so to speak, laying hold upon the broken pieces of your marred and spoiled life, and if you will let Him, He will now begin to complete your nature by making it to be what He meant it to be years ago when you were cradled at the foot of the cross.

Why have you failed? Because your life *is* a failure. You hide it by going to church, by observing the outward routine, by a hearty laugh, by a light, gay air. You live your life amongst your brethren or sisters, but no one knows that deep down in your soul you are certain that you are a failure, that you are spoiled, that you want things you do not obtain, that you long for a goodness you never realize, that you reach out for a sweetness and purity and strength that never comes. You know that your life has fallen beneath God's plan. You are ready to confess it. Why is it so? Is it because God has failed?

See that mother bending over the cradle where her firstborn babe lies. See how a smile lights up her face as she thinks she catches the plaudits which are to welcome his success in coming years. But no woman ever cherished for her babe visions half so fair as your God has for you. He hates nothing that He has made, and with an equal love He wants to do

HIS BEST FOR EACH.

What then is the cause? Is it that He has made a mistake in your life? You think so. If instead of being a poor man you had been rich, if instead of being a lone woman you had had one to call you wife, and little children to clutch your dress and call you mother; if instead of being tied to the office-stool you had been a minister or missionary, you think that you would have been a better, a sweeter character. But I want you to understand that God chose for you your lot in life out of myriads that were open to Him, because just where you are you might realize your noblest possibilities. Otherwise God would have made you different from what you are. But your soul, born into His kingdom, was a matter of care and thought to Him, how best He might nurture you; and He chose your lot with its irritations, its trials, its difficulties, all the agony that eats out your nature. Though men and women do not guess it, He chose it just as it is, because in it, if you will let Him, He can realize the fairest life within your reach.

Where is the failure? Look. I think I have the wheel before me. My foot is working the treadle. It is revolving rapidly, horizontally as you know. I have placed it on the clay. I begin to manipulate it. It rises beneath my hand till I come to one certain point where, either through some flaw in the clay, a bubble or a fault, it resists me. Leaving that point, I put my hand around again, and in some other direction endeavor to secure my purpose, and then come back to that one point, but again I meet that obstruction that thwarts me. The genius of my brain as an artist is complete; the power of my hand to manipulate is unrivaled; it is *the clay* that thwarts me, until presently, because I have been frustrated again and again, the work is a marred, spoiled thing.

Now is not that true of you?

The one trouble of my life, years ago, was just this about which I am speaking now. God was dealing with me. I suppose He wanted to make me a vessel fit for His use. But there was one point in my life where I fought God as the clay fights the hand of the potter. I fought God, I will not say for how long. God help me! the only benefit that I can get now out of those years the cankerworm has eaten, is to discover the secret in other lives while they too are standing still, and then to take them to the Christ to whom I went myself, and to encourage them to hope that He who years ago took up a spoiled and marred life and made a little of it, will take other men and women and will find out where they have thwarted Him; and finding it out, will touch them there, and as they yield to Him they will be made again.

Now what is the point in your life where you obstruct God? Allow me to search you.

WHERE IS IT?

People come to me and speak of the different points in which they have thwarted God. A man came to me one day and said that when I was in a certain convention I asked all those who wanted to be wholly for God to stand up. He refused to stand, and for months his will rose up and said, "Who is this man that I should stand up when he bids me?"

For months he fought this feeling, until not long ago he came to me and said, "Come and pray! I want to confess that I have been fighting the will of God for months, and I am wretched. Help me to get peace."

I was once staying with another man, a pastor. I had said nothing about smoking—I never do single out sins—I had not alluded to the habit; but one day we were walking along a street that led over a river, and to my surprise as we got to the apex of the bridge he took his tobacco-pouch and pipe and threw them over, and said, "There, I have settled that."

Then, turning to me, he said: "I know, Mr. Meyer,

you have said nothing about it; but for the last few months God has been asking me to set a new example to my young men, and I said, 'Why should not I do as I like, and they as they like? God was searching me, and I was fighting Him; but it is all settled now, sir, it is all done now."

A bright young girl, at the end of one of my addresses, was waiting about, and I said to her:

"Come, my girl, I am quite sure that you have got nothing to see me about."

"O," she said, "I have, sir. I remember that three or four years ago, when I was a girl at school, one of my companions asked me to go out and get some candy for her. I got it, but I kept back half the money for myself. That sin has been working in my mind. It seems as if God keeps saying, 'Confess, confess, restore'; but, sir, I have been fighting it for the last month or two. It looks so stupid to do a little thing like that."

I said, "My dear child, nothing is stupid that is going to please God and put you right with His will."

A man came to me and said, "I cannot understand it, sir, but it seems as if God is blotted out of my life. I used to be so happy."

I said, "How is it?"

Said he, "I think it has to do with my treatment of my brother. He served me cruelly over my father's will, and I said I would never forgive him. I am sorry I said it, but he has been going from bad to worse, has lost his wife and child, and is now on a bed of death, and I cannot go to him because I said I never would."

I said, "My friend, it is better to break a bad vow than keep it. Go."

He went, and the smile of God met him just there.

Sixteen years ago I was a minister in a Midland town in England, not at all happy, doing my work for the pay I got, but holding a good position amongst my fellows. Hudson Taylor and two young students came into my life. I watched them. They had something I had not. Those young men stood there in all their strength and joy. I said to Charles Studd, "What is the difference between you and me? You seem so happy, and I somehow am in the trough of the wave."

He replied, "There is nothing that I have got which you may not have, Mr. Meyer."

But I asked, "How am I to get it?"

"Well," he said, "have you given yourself right up to God?"

I winced. I knew that if it came to that, there was a point where I had been fighting my deepest convictions for months. I had lived away from it, but when I came to the Lord's table and handed out the bread and wine, then it met me; or when I came to a convention or meeting of holy people, something stopped me as I remembered this. It was the one point where my will was entrenched. I thought I would do something with Christ that night which would settle it one way or the other, and I met Christ. You will forgive a man who owes everything to one night in his life if to help other men he opens his heart for a moment. I knelt in my room and gave Christ the ring of my will with the keys on it, but kept one little key back, the key of a closet in my heart, in one back story in my heart. He said to me:

"Are they all here?"

And I said, "All but one."

"What is that?" said He.

"It is the key of a little cupboard," said I, "in which I have got something which Thou needest not interfere with, but it is mine."

Then, as He put the keys back into my hand, and seemed to be gliding away to the door, He said:

"My child, if you cannot trust Me with all, you do not trust Me at all."

I cried, "Stop," and He seemed to come back; and holding the little key in my hand, in thought I said:

"I cannot give it, but if Thou wilt take it Thou shalt have it."

He took it, and within a month from that time He had cleared out that little cupboard of things which had been there for months. I knew He would.

May I add one word more? Three years ago I met the thing I gave up that night, and as I met it I could not imagine myself being such a fool as nearly to have sold my birthright for that mess of pottage.

I looked up into the face of Christ and said, "Now I am thine." It seemed as if that was the beginning of a new ministry. The Lord got me on His wheel again, and He made me again, and He has been making me again ever since. I learned that night to say "yes," and I have tried to say "yes" ever since.

Now my friend, you say to me, "It is quite true, sir; my life is marred. But I am getting to be an old man. Do you think there is any hope for me?"

My text says: "He made it again."

Adelaide Proctor says, at the end of one of her verses, that we always may be what we might have been. In a sense that is not true. You and I never can recall the past, and yet—and yet Jesus has a wonderful knack of making men again.

There was Jacob, the supplanter, for instance. He met him again at the ford of Jabbok, and he was made into Israel, a prince of God. There was Peter, and He made him again so that on the day of Pentecost he became the means of the Holy Ghost's advent to the world. And he made again John Mark who went back before a touch of seasickness to his mother, but Paul said of him after, "Bring him, for he is profitable." He will make you again.

Canon Wilberforce told me that he had his likeness painted by the great artist Herkomer, who told him the following story. Herkomer was born in the Black Forest, his father a simple woodchopper. When the artist rose to name and fame in London, and built his studio at Bushey, his first thought was to have the old man come and spend the rest of his years with him. He came, and was very fond of molding clay. All day he made things out of clay, but as the years passed he thought his hand would lose its cunning. He often went upstairs at night to his room with the sad heart of an old man who thinks his best days are gone by. Herkomer's quick eyes of love detected this, and when his father was safe asleep his gifted son would come down stairs and take in hand the pieces of clay which his old father had left, with the evidences of defect and failure; and with his own wonderful touch he would make them as fair as they could be made by human hand. When the old man came down in the morning, and took up the work he had left all spoiled the night before, and held it up before the light, he would say, rubbing his hands, "I can do it as well as ever I did."

Is not that just what God Almighty is going to do with you? You are bearing the marks of failure just because you have been resisting Him and fighting Him. But, ah! my Lord comes with those pierced hands, and says, "Will you not yield to me? Only yield, and I will make you again."

There is a Pentecost for us all, but we must begin at the beginning. There must be the yielding.

Young girls who have come out of beautiful homes, the children of luxury, I tell you that all the exterior beauty of your life is only a faint adumbration and shadow of the infinite sweetness and grace of the life of Pentecost. Live in the promised land, men and women, you who have been seeking in the outside, in circumstances and things and people, your bliss.

YOU HAVE MISSED IT

—you always will that way. It is inside. It is in the Holy Ghost. It is in Christ. Heaven is there. It is there for all. But believe me, you cannot get it unless you take the preparatory step. Therefore you must get alone as I did sixteen years ago; you must kneel down before Christ and say:

"Christ, I give Thee my self, my will. With my will I yield to Thee. Thou art the Potter; I am the clay. Impose Thy will upon me."

And mind you, Christ will say to you, "What about this?" and if you can look up and say; "Yes, that is Thine." He will go forward and make you beautiful and happy. But if you refuse, you will stop there, you will be dwarfed, you will thwart Christ.

At Keswick, a little village in the Cumberland Hills, where we meet once a year to talk about these things, if you go out at ten o'clock, at eleven o'clock, at twelve o'clock, at one o'clock, you will see lights burning. My heart has often gone up in prayer because I know that every light means a Jabbok, and that at those places souls are yielding to God. At Northfield also a brother clergyman said to me, "Mr. Meyer, the work has not been done in the auditorium, but it has been done in the woods at night where we have gone to settle it with God."

Remember this. When I gave myself to God that night, the devil said, "Don't do it! If you let God have an inch, He will want an ell. If you yield in one thing you will have to yield in everything, and there is no knowing what you may not come to."

At first I thought there was something in it. Then I remembered my daughter, who was a little willful then, and loved her own way. I thought to myself as I knelt, "Supposing that she were to come and say—'Father, from tonight I am going to put my life into your hand; do with it what you will.' Would I call her mother to my side and say: 'Here is a chance to torment her. What would mortify her? What color dress does she hate? What companion does she detest? What method of spending her life does she abhor? Tell me, and I will put her through them all.' "

I knew I would not say that. I knew I would say to my wife, "Our child is going to follow our will from now. Do you know of anything that is hurting her?"

"Yes; so and so."
"Does she love it much?"
"Yes."
"Ah! she must give it up, but we will make it as easy for her as we can. We must take from her the things that are hurting her, but we will give her everything that will make her life one long summer day of bliss."

God will say that to you. He only takes that one thing away because it will hurt you. But oh! He will give, and give, and give! You have no idea what God will do for you. Say: "I am willing." But let me make a confession: I did not say that myself. I said, "I am not willing, O God, but I am willing to be made willing."

God help you to make the same prayer!

The Natural Man

IF IT WERE NOT that I believe in the Holy Ghost, I would almost shrink from speaking about the profound philosophy wherewith the apostle Paul deals with the self-life; but I believe that God's Spirit will take my broken words and speak to each of you.

Will you turn to I Corinthians 2:14: "The natural man receiveth not the things of the Spirit of God: for they are foolishness unto him: neither can he know them, because they are spiritually discerned."

"The natural man." The Greek is the "psychical" man, the man in whom the soul is all, and the spirit is like a dark, untenanted chamber.

The temple of old was constituted thus: outer court, holy place, holy of holies. The outer court corresponds to our body, the holy place to our soul, the holy of holies or the most holy place to our spirit. In the regenerate man the most holy place is tenanted by the Spirit of God, but in the unregenerate man it is untenanted and dark, waiting for its occupant. The natural man is the man whose spirit is empty of God.

In the fifteenth verse of the same chapter, we read: "But he that is spiritual judgeth all things, yet he himself is judged of no man."

Here we have the "spiritual" man, the man whose spirit is quick with the Spirit of God, who speaks and wills and lives beneath the impulse of the Holy Ghost Himself. Oh, that every believer became truly spiritual; spirit-unfilled (written with a small "s"): the Spirit of God (written with a large "S") dominating the spirit of man.

In the third chapter of the same epistle, Paul begins, "And I, brethren, could not speak unto you as unto spiritual, but as unto carnal, even as unto babes in Christ."

Now the "carnal" man is a Christian, a babe in Christ. We might think that the carnal man is unregenerate, but it is not so. He is regenerate, he is in Christ, and Christ is in him; but instead of Christ being predominant, the carnal element is predominant. I believe that there are hundreds of people who are in Christ; but they are babes in Christ. Christ is in them, but He is overcrowded by the superiority of their self-life. Their self-life was once clothed in rags; it is now clothed in the externals of religion; but it is still the self-life, and in the Christian may predominate over the Christ-life, and be the cause of unutterable darkness and sorrow.

May God help me now to reverse it, so that the carnal element shall be crowded out, shall be crucified, and the Christ element shall become the pivot of your life!

In order that you may know what the carnal element is, let me say that that word also stands for "flesh," and that the Greek word is *sarx*. Now the Apostle Paul uses the word *sarx* ("carnal" or "flesh") in a very especial form. He does not mean the natural body, but he means the element of self. That is proved from Romans 7:18, where he says, "In me, (that is, in my flesh), dwelleth no good thing." My flesh is "me." Some men spell it with a tiny *m,* and some with a capital *M,* but whether the *m* is in italics or in capitals, the "me" in each person is the flesh. Spell "flesh" backwards, drop the *h,* as we are apt to do in London, and you get s-e-l-f; "flesh" is "self," and "self" is "flesh." It is "me," and as long as "me" is first and Christ second, I am living a carnal life though I am in Christ and a saved man.

FOUR CHARACTERISTICS OF THE CARNAL LIFE

Now the carnal life is *a babe life.* What is sweeter than a babe? So beautiful, so wee, one can take the child so close to oneself. But what is tender and beautiful in a babe for a few months is terrible at the end of twelve months, or ten years. And what is lovely in a young convert is terrible in a man of ten or twenty years of Christian life. I have met men who use the same expressions twenty years after conversion that they did when they were cradled on Calvary; and if you are still living in the elementary stage of experience and feeling and prayer, and do not grow, do not know God better, do not know the Bible better, do not know yourself better, do not know Christ better, you are a little babe, you are carnal.

And then the carnal man *lives on milk.* Paul said, "I have fed you with milk, and not with meat: for hitherto ye were not able to bear it, neither yet now are ye able." Milk is food which has passed through the digestion of another. The babe cannot take meat, so the mother takes meat, and breaks it down, and the child takes milk. So many Christians cannot read the Bible, cannot get any good out of the Bible, it must be broken down by their minister, and they are fed with a spoon! Ministers are nurses. They have to spend their time wheeling the converts about, comforting them, putting them to sleep, waking them up and feeding them; and if they are not fed with a spoon three or four times a week, there is no knowing what will happen. And if you are in that state that you must take spiritual truth through the digestion of another, you are a babe.

A carnal Christian is also *sectarian*. "I am of Paul, and I am of Apollos, and I of Cephas." Oh, how much we make of the fold, and how little of the flock! How much we think of the hurdles, and how little of the sheep! One man says, "I am a Baptist"; and another, "I am a Presbyterian"; a third says, "I am a Roman Catholic"; and a fourth, "I am evangelical." Half the time we are worrying about the sect to which we belong. Directly a man begins in that course, and forgets the Church with a large C—the Church of Christ—he is a carnal Christian and a babe.

I would lead you one step further because I desire to make my system perfectly clear. Turn to Hebrews 5:14, where we read:

"Strong meat belongeth to them that are of full age, even those who by reason of use have their senses exercised to discern both good and evil."

Here we have a fourth characteristic of the carnal Christian: such an one is *unable to exercise his senses to discern good and evil*. When I returned to England from one of my Atlantic voyages, my nose was very sensitive: the pure ozone of the Atlantic had made me very keen to discern impurity. I went to stay with some friends in the country, and all that time I was haunted by a noisome effluvia. I said, "What is the matter?"

"Oh," they said, "there is nothing wrong."

I said, "I am sure there is," and presently, after investigating, about a mile off we discovered a sewage-farm which infected the air. My friends who had had no training on the Atlantic were unable to detect it. So there are men who take up a novel full of impure thought and read it and not feel hurt, though the hurt has been certainly received; men and women who listen to uncharitable talk, and not detect its undertone; men and women who go in and out in the world and mix in its pleasure and sin, and still call themselves Christians, because they cannot discern good and evil.

Those four tests,—are they true of you? I am here as a surgeon, and must help you to anatomize yourself to know where you are. Are you growing? Are you living on the strong meat of the Bible? Are you a sectary? Have you the power to discriminate between good and evil? By these four tests you may know whether the Christ-life or the flesh-life is predominant in you.

Let us go deeper. When God created man, He gave all intelligent beings a self-hood, a power of self-determination. He gave it to angels. Demons have it, because they were angels. Men have it—selfhood. The Creator meant the selfhood to be dependent on Himself, so that a Christian might turn to the Creator and say, "Live Thou in Thy will through me." When Jesus Christ, the perfect man, came among men, during all His earthly life He said nothing and willed nothing from Himself; He lived a truly dependent life. The vegetable creation—flowers, the trees—they depend on God absolutely, and that makes them so beautiful. Consider the lilies and the cedars, how they grow! And the angels who have kept their first estate live on God. God wills, thinks, acts, energizes through them. Satan was once an archangel dependent on God, but something passed over him and he caught the fever of independence, and began to make himself his own pivot; and so he began to be in hell; because hell is the assertion of self to the exclusion of God, and heaven is the assertion of God to the exclusion of self. The devil fell, and all his crew that leaned on him, instead of on God, fell also. Then when man was made, Satan traversed the abyss, and whispered to man, "Be God, be independent, take your own way, do your own will."

Man in his fall withdrew his nature from dependence upon God, and made himself a center of his own life and activity. And this world is cursed to-day because men and women are living for self, and the flesh-life. The carnal mind is enmity against God, and is darkness and despair.

Christianity is a science, a deep science, which tries to do away with the evil or the fall into selfishness by substituting for self the Son of God, which is Christ. Is it not wonderful that Hinduism and Christianity are each of them intended to deal with the same root of evil? But the Hindu tries to exterminate the self-life by absorption in eternity until Nirvana sets in, while the Christian who also sees that the self-life is accursed eliminates it by the philosophy and the action which I am now going to describe.

SELF-WILL SHOWS ITSELF IN VARIOUS FORMS.

"Now the works of the flesh are manifest, which are these: Adultery, fornication, uncleanness, lasciviousness, idolatry, witchcraft, hatred, variance, emulations, wrath, strife, seditions, heresies, envyings, murders, drunkenness, revelings, and such like." There you have the passion of the self-life in lust. "Are ye so foolish? having begun in the Spirit are ye now made perfect by the flesh?" There you have the aspirations of the self-life, trying to perfect itself. There was a school of perfection in Galatia, and they sought to perfect themselves in their own energy; and there have been schools of perfection since then which have tried to be good in the energy of the self-life. "Let no man beguile you of your reward in a voluntary humility and worshiping of angels, intruding into those things which he hath not seen, vainly puffed up by his fleshly mind, and not holding the Head, from which all the body by joints and bands having nourishment ministered, and knit together, increaseth with the increase of God." There you have some intellectualism prying into the things of God, but not submitting to the will of God and the teaching of God. "When I therefore was thus minded, did I use lightness? or the things that I purpose, do I purpose according to the flesh, that with me there should be yea, yea, and nay, nay?" There you have the self-life planning, scheming, and arranging for itself, and the Apostle says: "I am not going to plan after the flesh."

We see then that we are always in danger of doing good things from the self pivot. That is our curse. I hear of a man who has consecrated himself to God, and

I say to myself: "I will do the same." I hear of a man who has attracted crowds by some special lantern, or by some new machinery, and I say: "I too will do the same." I learn of a school which is teaching a certain line of doctrine, and because I think it will pay, and get me prestige and popularity I adopt it. But not until I begin to notice the working of my own life, shall I have any conception how perpetually the self-life is underlying all.

HOW TO GET RID OF THE SELF-LIFE

I will show you. There are *three steps*: the cross, the Spirit, the contemplation of the risen Christ. May we take them now; may the Spirit of God reveal to each one this blessed secret!

First, the cross. Now understand that I hold that on the cross Jesus Christ offered a substitutionary sacrifice for the sins of the whole world. But there is a second meaning significant in the cross. Turn to Romans 8:3, 4: "What the law could not do in that it was weak through the flesh, God sending His own Son in the likeness of sinful flesh, and for sin, condemned sin in the flesh: that the righteousness of the law might be fulfilled in us, who walk not after the flesh but after the Spirit." God sent His own Son in the likeness of sinful flesh, and for sin. "For sin" is substitutionary. "In the likeness of sinful flesh" is the reference of the cross to sanctification. On the cross God nailed in the person of Christ the likeness of our sinful flesh. I cannot explain it to you more than that; but I know this—that next to seeing Jesus as my sacrifice, nothing has revolutionized my life like seeing the effigy of my sinful self in the sinless, dying Saviour. I say to myself:

"God has nailed the likeness of my self-life to the cross. The cross is the symbol of degradation and curse. Cursed is everyone that hangs on the cross. If then God has treated the likeness of my sinful self, when borne by the sinless Christ, as worthy of His curse, how terrible in God's sight it must be for myself to hug it and embrace it and live in it!"

Oh, wondrous cross! But that is not all.

Christ and I are one. In Him I hung there. I came to an end of myself in Christ, and kneeling at His cross I took the position of union with Him in His death, and I consigned my self-life to the cross. It was as though I took my self-life with its passions, its choices, its yearnings after perfection, its wallowing, its fickleness, its judgment of others, its uncharity—I took it as a felon, and said:

"Thou art cursed, thou shalt die. My God nailed thee to that cross. Come, thou shalt come. I put thee there by my choice, by my will, by my faith. Hang there."

After that moment—you remember in Galatians it is the aorist tense: "They that are Christ's, crucified the flesh with its affections and lusts"—after that moment, that decisive in my life, I have ever reckoned that my self-life is on the cross, and that the death of Christ lies between me and it.

Let me make that perfectly clear. Supposing a woman has been married to a felon, a drunkard, a libertine. After years of sorrow there comes a moment of liberty when she seeks and obtains a divorce. She now enters into union with a perfectly lovely blessed man who becomes to her everything. Whenever her former husband reels along the street and seeks to get her back into his power, she points to a moment, the moment when the divorce was granted, and she says, "From that moment I became divorced from you. Touch me if you dare."

If he comes reeling across the street, she only clutches closer the arm of the true man she loves, and puts him on the other side between the sot and herself. She counts from the moment of deliverance.

Now think about it, pray about it. Later I am going to publish the marriage-bans between you and Christ, and to show how Christ takes the place of self. But we must move together, my friends. You must allow me to be persistent. You will not benefit by this teaching unless you act as the result of any separate address in the direction it indicates. So kneel down before the cross of Jesus, and realize why your Christian life has been a failure. The cause of your darkness and sorrow and desertion is to found here: you have never consigned the self-life where God consigned it. In your will, with streaming eyes, with reverent face, unite yourself with the death of Christ. Doing só, remember you will do what Jesus said Peter must do. Peter said, "Thou art the Christ."

"Well and good," Christ replied. "I am going to die."

Peter said, "You must not think of it. Spare Thyself."

Ah, that is what you will hear said to you a thousand times—spare thyself!

Jesus said, "Get thee behind me. That is Satan: it is

the spirit of the pit. If a man will come after me, let him deny himself, and take up his cross and follow me."

You may say what you like about Christianity, but I undertake to affirm it has been shamefully misrepresented, both by Protestant and by any other class of Christians. They have thought that Christianity depended in the objective, whereas it is subjective largely, equally. They have thought that it depended on trusting Christ to put away your sin, whereas it also consists in trusting Christ to deliver you from yourselves, who are the center and curse of your life.

Whenever the self-life obtrudes, reckon yourself dead to it; reckon that the cross stands between you and it.

But you say, "Sir, I do not see how I am to live like that. I shall always be on pins and needles, always in agony whether this is self or not, and I do not see how I am to live."

Ah, I thought you would say that! I said that myself, and here comes the *second* point: the Holy Spirit.

"If ye through the Spirit do mortify the deeds of the body, ye shall live." And again, "The Spirit lusteth against the flesh."

It was by the Eternal Spirit that Christ offered Himself without spot to God, and it is by the Eternal Spirit that the cursed spirit of self is going to be antagonized in your life and mine. Just as in a scarlet-fever case you use carbolic acid, and the carbolic acid antagonizes the germs of disease, so turning from that curse I kneel before the Holy Ghost, and say, "Spirit of God, infill, *infill,* INFILL my entire being, deeper, deeper, deeper yet. In the depth of my nature, when I am least thinking about it, go on day by day as the antiseptic of my flesh or self-life. Antagonize it, work against it, keep it out of sight, keep it under Christ."

The Holy Ghost will do it.

But you say, "Mr. Meyer, I am so afraid that if I am always dealing with the self-life, it will hurt me. It will be like standing by a bier and seeing death disintegrate a corpse."

This leads me to my *third* point, and I reply—and this is the beauty of it—that while the Spirit of God in the depth of your heart is antagonizing the self-life, He does it by making Jesus Christ a living, bright reality. He fixes your thoughts upon Jesus. You do not think about the Spirit, you hardly think about self, but you think much about your dear Lord; and all the time that you are thinking about Him, the process of disintegration and dissolution and death of self is going on within your heart.

A dear sister said to me once, "I am going to spend a whole day praying for the Holy Ghost."

She went to a hut in a wood, and she came back to me at night and said, "I have had a grand day, but I am a bit disappointed. I do not feel that I have more of the Holy Ghost now than I did."

"But," I said, "is Jesus much to you?"

"Oh," she replied, "Jesus never was so sweet and precious as He is now."

"Why, my dear woman," I said, "that is the Holy Ghost, because He glorifies Christ, and when the Holy Ghost works most, you do not think about the Holy Ghost, but you think about your dear Lord."

O, man and woman, forgive me! It is a very broken,

broken way of putting the deepest mystery in the Bible, but I can only ask that the Holy Spirit may make you know what it is to have Jesus as the center and origin of your life. The fountain and origin hitherto has been self, has it not? O cursed self, Barabbas, Barabbas, to the cross! The world says: "Not Christ, but Barabbas, self." The Christian says: "Not Barabbas, but Christ."

May God explain this to you, for His name's sake.

The Substitution of the Christ-Life for the Self-Life

IN MY SECOND ADDRESS we saw that the will is our main and chief impediment. We are not what we *feel,* or *think,* or *wish,* but what we *will*. In the preceding address we saw that our curse lies in making self the pivot of our life, and that the one aim of Christianity is to put Christ where man puts self. I want now to show shortly, concisely, with the power of God's Spirit who cooperates, how this may be done, and I am going to use the Epistle to the Galatians.

In Galatians 5:19, we have the works of self: "Adultery, fornication, uncleanness, lasciviousness, idolatry, witchcraft, hatred, variance, emulations, wrath, strife, seditions, heresies, envyings, murders, drunkenness, revelings, and such like." Wherever man's nature works itself out, the lust of the flesh shows itself in every casino, saloon and house of ill-fame.

Turn to Galatians 3:3: "Are ye so foolish? Having begun in the Spirit, are ye now made perfect by the flesh?" Will you be made perfect in the flesh? In the regenerate man, the church-member, there is the same principle of self-life; and though you do not find him in a den of drink or lust or infamy, the same principle which is working unrestrained and unbridled there is working in his heart also. He gives to the collection, to the subscription list, that men may see how much he gives. He seeks to please God by prayer, by the communion, by ritualistic observances. He will even try to be perfect. There is many a man who goes to Keswick and to Northfield, trying to pile up his religious life in the energy of his religious-looking self. But I repeat it: the curse of the Christian and of the world is that self is our pivot; it is because Satan made self his pivot that he became a devil. Take heaven from its center in God, and try to center it in self, and you transform heaven into hell. I know little or nothing about the fire, or the darkness, or the worm of hell. Hell is selfishness, and selfishness is hell. And

THE PHILOSOPHY OF THE BIBLE

is to do away with self, and to make Christ all in all.

When I am dealing with a drunkard I am inclined to say to him, "Be a man."

What a fool I am! I am trying to cast out the evil of drink by the evil of self-esteem. If I want to save a man, I must cast out the spirit of self, and substitute the Lord Jesus Christ. Alpha, Omega, all in all.

But how? How?

This epistle to the Galatians is my battle-axe. Luther used it for justification, but I think it is for sanctification.

How? By the cross, and by the cross as presented in the Epistle to the Galatians.

The Apostle tells us in Galatians 1:4: "Jesus Christ, who gave Himself for our sins, that He might deliver us from this present evil world, according to the will of God and our Father." He considers the cross in its aspect toward sanctification. He says: "He delivered us from this present evil world." In Romans we have the cross for justification, the putting-away of sin; in Galatians for sanctification, the cross standing between me and my past, between me and the world, between me and myself: the cross, and I count from that cross. That is the ground taken in Galatians.

Take Galatians 2:20: "I have been crucified with Christ." God demands that every man and woman should unite with the cross, and (so to speak) kill the self-life, the egotism, the personal element which has been so strong in each one. Not your individuality, however. Isaiah will still be Isaiah, and Malachi, Malachi; but the proud, fussy self-esteem, yourself, ego, the flesh, must be crucified. Christ denied His divine self, and you and I must deny our fallen self. Christ's temptation was to use His divine attribute; your temptation is that you should use your human attribute. You must put it to the cross, and believe that from this moment it shall be crucified to you and you to it. Barabbas to the cross, to the cross! Christ, come down from the cross and live in here!

Galatians 5:24: The aorist: "They that are Christ's crucified the flesh." Galatians 6:14: "God forbid that I should glory save in the cross of our Lord Jesus Christ, by whom the world is crucified unto me, and I unto the world." The world looks at me as a felon, but I have my revenge. That by which I am crucified to the world, by that the world is crucified to me. It may say what it likes about me. I retaliate, "Take it back; it is all true of thyself."

This wonderful epistle speaks of the cross as between me and Egypt, between me and the wilderness, between me and my past, my wanderings; and now the cross is my Jordan by which I pass through death into the land where Joshua leads, the land that flows with milk and honey.

This epistle also treats of the Holy Ghost, because as I have said before, it is only the Holy Spirit that can make your reckoning true. You choose the cross, but the Holy Spirit as it were mortifies, makes dead, makes real. *You* reckon, *He* makes real your reckoning. And hence Galatians 5:17: "The flesh lusteth against the Spirit, and the Spirit against the flesh: and these are contrary the one to the other: so that ye cannot do the things that ye would." Galatians 5:16: *"Walk* in the Spirit"; 5:18: *"Be led* of the Spirit"; 5:25: *"Live* in the Spirit." And while you walk in the Spirit, are led of the Spirit, and live in the Spirit, the Holy Spirit will go on lusting and agonizing and making real to you your reckoning of death.

You have not therefore got to worry about the death side; think about the life side. Do not live looking at the corpse, but live looking to the Holy Ghost; and as you trust Him for every movement, as you breathe in the Holy Ghost moment by moment as you breathe in air, in the depth of your heart He will draw you away from the flesh, the self, the world, the devil; and insensibly, unconsciously, exquisitely, He will bring you into life. And the more you live on the life side, the more, without knowing much of it, you will live on the death side; for while you are engrossed with the Holy Ghost, the Holy Ghost in the depth of your being is carrying the sentence of death deeper, deeper, deeper down, and things are being mortified of which you once had no conception.

Now listen: If you choose the cross, if you live in the Spirit, the Spirit lusts (always the present tense), lusteth against the flesh. I do not know how your Bible reads, but some Bibles are printed wrong. "The flesh lusteth against the Spirit, and the Spirit against the flesh," and "Spirit" is spelled with a small *s*. Take some ink and alter that. It is not "spirit" with a small *s;* it is "Spirit" with a capital *S,* the Holy Spirit. "The flesh, the self, lusts against the Holy Spirit, and the Holy Spirit lusts against the flesh."

Now, let us look at *five texts in Galatians* on the inner life, the indwelling of Christ.

1. Galatians 1:15, 16: "When it pleased God, who separated me from my mother's womb, and called me by His grace, to reveal His Son in me, that I might preach Him among the heathen; immediately I conferred not with flesh and blood." "It pleased God to reveal His Son in me." Now, "to reveal" means "to undrape." There is a statue. It is covered with a veil. It is there, but hidden. I take off the veil, and you see it. When you were regenerate, Christ came unto you; that is what regeneration means—Christ born into your spirit. But Christ came in as a veiled figure, and you who are regenerate but who have never seen the Christ as I put Him before you in the last address, you have Christ in you, but He is veiled. Now, mark. When Jesus died, the veil of the temple was rent in twain from the top to the bottom; and when the soul appreciates the death of Christ as its own death to sin, the veil is rent in twain from the top to the bottom, and the Holy Ghost reveals Jesus as the Substitute for the self-life.

"It pleased God to reveal His Son in me." O, my God, I thank Thee that Thou hast revealed Thy Son as the Alpha, the pivot, the fountain, the origin of my life! May it be so with us all!

A friend of mine was staying near Mont Blanc. He had been there for a fortnight, but had not seen the "monarch of the Alps." Nearly out of heart with waiting, he was preparing to leave. Going up to dress for dinner, he passed a window and saw that the monarch was still veiled in mist. Having dressed, he came downstairs, passing the window again. Every vestige of mist had now parted, and Mont Blanc stood revealed from base to snow-clad peak. So now there shall come upon you a breath of the Holy Ghost, before which the misconception of your life shall pass, and to you God will reveal His Son in you as the center of your life.

Turn for a moment to Colossians 1:27, a very favorite passage: "To whom God would make known what is the riches of the glory of this mystery among the Gentiles; which is Christ in you, the hope of glory."

A woman sits alone. Her son ran away to sea twenty years ago. She is a widow, poor, lonely. A bronzed stranger comes.

"Can I sleep in your spare room?"

"I have a room to let, so you can stay."

He comes in disguised, so that she cannot see him. He is there, but she knows him not. One day they sit together at dinner, and there is a gesture, and she says, "John!"

That is the glory of the mystery when the two kiss.

"My boy!"

"My mother!"

Then after dinner he says: "Mother, you shall never lack again. Here is gold. I am going to live with you, never to go away again."

That is the riches of the glory of the mystery of her boy in the house.

Jesus, come! You have come, but You are a mystery. But we have come to the cross, and the mystery is gone, and there is the glory of the day; but there will be the riches of the glory of the mystery, Christ in us; and He will do for us better than ever we could have done for ourselves.

2. Galatians 1:24: "They glorified God in me." Some young men belonging to the Salvation Army came to old Andrew Bonar and said, "Dr. Bonar, we have been all night with God. Can't you see our faces shine?"

The old man said, "Moses wist not that his face shone."

When you have got the real article you do not need to advertize it, the public will come for it; but the man who has got what we call in England, brummagem ware, a sham, must puff it. If you have got Christ in you, people will not glorify you, they will glorify Christ in you, and they will say, "Teach us about Christ who has made you so fair."

"They glorified God in me." Dear brother ministers, when you get this, they will not glorify your sermons, they will not glorify your intellect, and they will not glorify your eloquence; but they will glorify God who shines through you as the Shekinah shone through the temple of old.

3. Galatians 2:8: "The same was mighty in me." Hudson Taylor told me that on the threshold of his

great life-work God came to him and said, "My child, I am going to evangelize inland China, and if you like to walk with me I will do it through you."

"Mighty in me." I cannot take that Bible class, but Christ is in me, and HE can. I cannot conduct that mission, but Christ is in me, and HE can. I cannot assume these responsibilities, but hallelujah! it does not matter. A copper wire has only to convey the message, it is for the battery to send it; and you may be forever more like the wire which connects you with cities far down its course, the wire along which the fair and the false passes without fret, without anxiety, without care; a mighty, mighty force meeting in the wire. When it is not self but Christ, it is Christ "mighty in me."

4. Galatians 2:20: "Christ liveth in me." One day when traveling by train, a young man sat opposite me in the car, reading Thomas à Kempis' *Imitation of Christ*. I knew the book, and sat beside him and said, "A grand book."

He said, "Yes."

Said I, "I have found something better."

"Better?"

"Yes."

"How?"

"Better for me, because I was always a poor hand at imitation. I imitated the minister with whom I settled from college, and nobody but myself and my wife ever guessed that my sermons were imitations of his. When I was a boy, my father had me taught drawing, and my master put before me something, and my copy needed to have letter-press underneath to state it was an imitation of the copy. And when I sat down to imitate Christ, no one could have guessed what I was trying to attain. "But," said I, "my young friend, if my drawing-master could have infused the spirit of his skill into my brain and hand, he could have drawn through me as fair a drawing as his own; and if my great and noble friend could have only put his spirit into me, why should I not have spoken even as he? And if instead of imitating Christ far away in the glory, He will come by the Holy Ghost and dwell in me, by His grace He shall work through my poor yielded life, a life something like His own fair life." Christ liveth in me.

Many have no idea what religion is. Re-ligion, *re-ligo,* a Latin word meaning "I bind,"—it is the binding of the heart to the Lord. No, I recall that; it is better: "He that is joined to the Lord is one spirit." O Christ, Thou art one with me, to make me one with Thee world without end!

5. One verse more. Galatians 4:19: "My little children, of whom I travail in birth again until Christ be formed in you." You know, of course, that an egg has in it a little embryo of life, and the nutriment the viscous fluid upon which it shall grow; and every day the little life germ pecks into this more and more, and the chick is formed in the shell. Until now there has been a good deal more of other elements in your life than of Christ, but from now the Christ is going to grow and increase and absorb into Himself everything else, and be formed in you.

Brother ministers, will you forgive that I have stated the truths of Christ's holy gospel so imperfectly? How can human words tell what Christ is prepared to be? But let me entreat you to pass by a great deal of political life, and it may be, (though it is not wrong), of the social life around you; and I charge you to live to preach the deep philosophy of the indwelling Christ, and let men know what Jesus meant when He said, "In that day ye shall know that I am in the Father, and ye in me, and I in you."

Christ the Complement of Our Need

WE HAVE NOW DEALT with the will, and have seen that our curse is the self-life. We have also learned that Jesus Christ can take the place of self. I want now to show what Jesus Christ can be, and may the Holy Spirit glorify Christ!

I Corinthians 10:11: "Now all these things happened unto them for ensamples: and they are written for our admonition, upon whom the ends of the world are come."

Once we were in Egypt. Everyone who has been redeemed by the blood of Christ was once in Egypt. Egypt stands for three things: (1) sensual pleasure, leeks, garlics, onions; (2) bondage, the taskmaster, the brick, and the treasure city; and (3) anguish of soul. I suppose there is not one now in Christ that does not remember the sensual pleasure, the bondage and the anguish of soul. Out of that God has brought us. He brought us when He brought Christ through death to resurrection, and He brought us when each one (as it were) was sheltered beneath the Paschal Lamb, and the blood spoke to God. O blessed moment when we entered into peace, when we put the blood upon the door-post and the lintel, and because God saw the blood we were ransomed, and in joy went forth from the land of bondage!

And as we stood upon the further shore of the Red Sea we repeated Miriam's Song, we rejoiced in God our Saviour. We gave ourselves up to follow the cloud, we sheltered beneath it by day and by night. We depended upon God for everything—for the water that gushed from the rock, and the manna that fell upon the desert floor. O happy, happy, happy days when we, fresh redeemed and with the consciousness of liberty, walked with God in the first hours of our conversion!

Then we came beneath Sinai. We obtained a new thought of God's holiness and righteousness, and as we first came there we said with all the fervor of a true intention: "Whatever God says, we will do." But our joy began to pass away, for as we tried to keep the law of God we fell hour by hour into sin that we loathed. It was the experience of the seventh chapter of Romans. After the inward man we loved the law of God, but when we came to do what we would we found we could not. We were like men raised from some illness, who know how to walk perfectly well, but when they begin they totter, and presently fall to the ground.

After staying there, we heard the command of God to arise and depart, and after some days we came to Kadesh-barnea. Now Kadesh is on the frontier of the land of Canaan. At Kadesh the rolling prairie sinks into the sand and waste of the desert. At Kadesh you looked back on Egypt, and forward into Palestine. To Kadesh there came spies, bringing in their hands baskets full of fruit which they had gathered in the Land of Promise, grapes, pomegranates, apricots, sweet and luscious fruit. At Kadesh you passed them round, you ate, you said, "It is a good land."

Many of you have been to Kadesh. You took lodgings there—at Northfield, at Keswick conventions; and men who have been over into the Land of Promise came back, and in their addresses and books they gave you a basket of fruit, and you said: "It is very good."

But there you stopped, and instead of going over the frontier and living in the land, you have gone

BACK TO THE DESERT.

Why did Israel stop there? Because she did not believe God. She believed that God could bring her from Egypt, but she could not believe that God could bring her to Canaan. She believed in the God of the past, but she could not believe in the God of every moment. She had an evil heart of unbelief, and departed from the living God.

You believe in Calvary, but not in the ascension. You believe in Christ who died, but not in Christ who rose and lives. You believe in conversion as a past fact, but you have no idea that He who converted you is prepared hour by hour to bring you into and to keep you in the Land of Rest.

The wilderness stands for three things.

First. Restlessness; a redeemed people, but restless. There is a chapter in Numbers, and thirty-three times in it we are told that the people removed. That has been your life for years, to and fro, trying this church and that, this minister and that minister, but all the while certain that you have not got God's rest.

Secondly. It stands for discontent; they murmured. And what a murmuring life yours is! You have got riches, love, happy, happy surroundings, but there is always something that you want altered. Discontent! If it is summer, it is too hot. If it is winter, it is too cold. If you have love you want money, and if you have money you want love. Backwards and forwards, full of restless murmuring and discontent. That has been your life as a Christian.

Thirdly. It stands for back-yearning, yearning backwards. The people had come out of Egypt, but they were always thinking about it. And your life is a negative life. You are out of Egypt, but you go as near Egypt as you can, and you look over into the pleasures of Egypt, you look over into the doings of Egypt, you look over into the passions and sins of Egypt, and though you are out of it your heart hungers after it. You are a Christian, but a worldly man has a happier time than you, for the worldly man has never had a glimpse of what you have. He is contented. You have enough religion to make you wretched.

What next? You came to Jordan. The poet has taught us to think that Jordan means death, the death of the body; but that is a false conception. In God's imagery the Jordan stands for death, but not the death of the body; but death to the self-life. I trust I have made it clear that I do not believe that self ever dies. I do not believe in the eradication of self, but I believe we come to the cross, to Jordan, and we put the cross, the death of Christ, between ourselves and our past life. We pass through the Jordan in our own experience when we unite ourselves with Christ's death, and are planted with Him in the likeness of His death. After that we stand in the land of Canaan.

At Kadesh you looked over, but now you are in. You

do not feel much. When you awoke you thought you would feel joy, but it is not so. You are quiet and still. Never mind! A man may cross the equator and not know it. The equator is marked on the map, but not on the ocean, and a man may cross it and not know it. Without emotion or passion, relying upon the Holy Ghost to make your reckoning true, you have passed Jordan, you are now in the land.

AND WHAT IS THE LAND?

The land is Christ. Canaan is Christ. He is the Land of Promise. Those mountains are the mountains of His strength. Those valleys are His humility. Those springs are His joy. Those rivers are His Holy Spirit. Those treasures are His wealth. That land—look at it! It is all yours. It is Christ in you, and you in Christ—that is Paradise.

That is proved by Hebrews 3:14: "We are made partakers of Christ." The third chapter of Hebrews is the wilderness experience. The fourth chapter is the Christ possession; and the Apostle says that we who believe are made to partake of Christ. Christ in us, Christ around us, Christ in the glory! I want to talk to you about that.

The first thing to do is to *get to know the land*. I remember when I was in Chicago someone told me that a family may purchase, or obtain from your Government, a farm in the far West. Gathering their goods together, a father, mother, and children will travel in the caravan (as we would call it in England), to the far West. They will sit in their house on the edge of their inheritance while the father surveys it. Leaving his wife and children, he climbs the mountain, and looks that way and this way, down to the river, away to the mountain; and all that tract is his. He walks to and fro. He says to himself: "It is a good land." He comes back home, and says to his wife, "Wife, we have got a grand inheritance."

That is the first thing he does.

The second is this. He gets some hurdles, and stakes off a part, and cultivates it. Next year he pushes the hurdles back, and takes more and cultivates that, and year after year he pushes the hurdles further back, until at last in twenty years his hurdles have reached the extent of his territory, and he has brought the whole of it under cultivation.

Now come with me. Come climb this mountain, the mountain of the Holy Ghost's teaching, and (1) *see what a Christ we have got;* and before I close we will encircle a little bit of Christ, we will (2) *take Him.* To-morrow we will push the hurdle further out, and take more of Christ, and the day after more, and the week after more, and year after year more. Only in eternity you will never put your fence of occupation on the margin of Christ's fullness, for when you have gone your furthest, still Christ will be eternally more.

Now see what Christ is. Look at I Corinthians 2:12: "That we might know the things that are freely given to us of God."

They tell me that George Macdonald, wanting to teach his children honor and truth and trust, places on the mantleshelf of the common room in their house, money enough for the whole use of his family. If the wife wants money she goes for it, if the boys and girls want money they go for it; whatever want there is in that house is supplied from that mantel-shelf deposit. So

God put in Jesus everything the soul can want, and He says, "Go and take it. It is all there for you."

Are you in sorrow? In Christ there is joy. Are you tempted? In Christ there is succor. Are you at the end of your strength? In Jesus there is might. I recall those words, however, because you might think that God gives this or that apart from Christ. Let me put it more correctly so: you take Christ to be whatever you want, and He is the supply of your want, your need, so that you are blessed with all spiritual blessings in Christ in heavenly places. All that you want is in Christ, and I think it is a good thing to want in order to learn what there is in Christ.

I remember when I was a boy my mother never took so much notice of me as when I was disappointed and weak and ill and worn. I think sometimes I used to sham a bit because my mother always did so much for me then. It is when you are weak and weary, and your faith has gone, and your strength is exhausted, and your hopes are vanishing, and everything around is passing from your grasp—it is then that God comes and says, "Child, I have put into Jesus everything your spirit wants"; and though, like Madam Guyon, you have to spend ten years in jail, Christ will be friends and comfort and strength and society, and all you want.

Would that people might understand what Jesus can be to the soul—these people who have been going into society, to the play, to the opera, to worldly pleasure, into the old past, thinking that they must obtain peace and joy in them, and they are only disappointed! Would that I could tell them that in Jesus they have mountains and lakes and rivers and streams and treasures and cornfields and olive yards, and everything a soul can want to make it blessed! Spirit of God, take of the things of Christ and reveal them to every waiting heart!

I now want you to see

HOW TO TAKE

because John says that of His fullness we have all *received,* and Paul says that they which *receive* abundance of life shall reign. RECEIVE.

Do you know how to receive? You say, "Sir, I suppose you mean, I need to pray."

No sir, I do not mean that. You have been praying long enough. I want you to leave off praying in a sense, and to begin taking. There is all the difference in the world between praying for Christ and taking Christ. I will explain. Years ago, I was staying with Canon Wilberforce at Southampton—it was in the first flush of my new surrender. One autumn night he said, "We will sit around the fire and give our experiences."

Lord Radstock sat next to me, and he commenced. I followed, and talked as a young convert to this great teaching will talk—a good deal about my surrender to Christ. An old clergyman who sat on the other side of the circle, arose and said, "I am very startled that Mr. Meyer has nothing better than that. To hear him talk you would suppose that we had only got to give up. Now my religion is *taking in,* taking in first, and dropping and giving up afterwards."

When you get gold you part with dross, and when you get real diamonds you part with paste. Get Christ, and the world attracts you no more. Give me sunlight, and I will dispense with electric light. Give me the light of day, I need no artificial luminary.

He continued, "I used once to be overcome by temper. I fought against temper. I came to the end of myself one afternoon when a number of children refused to listen to my teaching. I was on the point of losing my temper, when I turned to Christ, and said, 'Christ, be my sweet temper.'"

Instead of fighting against bad temper, he took Christ to be his patience, his humility, his meekness, his self-control. I saw in a moment that it was a better experience. I remember next morning when Canon Wilberforce came downstairs, as we stood together he said, "What did you think of that last night?"

I replied, "I think it will mark an era in my life."

He said, "It will do the same in mine."

From that moment I have tried to live that way, and whatever I have needed, I have said, "Christ, be this in me." That is the good fruit of the land.

Will you take this? Jesus does love you. Jesus is always near you. I do not talk about the cross so much as about Jesus who was crucified. I do not talk about the grave, but about Jesus who rose. I do not talk about the ascension, but about Jesus who ascended. He is with you and me always. It is not holiness, but it is Jesus the holy one. It is not meekness, it is Jesus the meek one. It is not purity, it is Jesus the pure one, Jesus, Jesus, Jesus! not *it,* not an *experience,* not *emotion,* not *faith,* but JESUS.

You have been worrying about your faith. Give it up! Do not think about your faith; think about Jesus, and you will have faith without knowing it. You have been worrying about your feeling. It does not matter, it goes up and down with the barometer. Have done with it, and live in the presence of Jesus.

Soul, thou and Jesus are standing face to face. Give thy whole self to Him and He gives His whole self to thee. Go to your bare garret, go to your dying child, go to scenes of trouble and sorrow and pain. He goes too. You have got the fountain beside you. You do not need to take your pitcher and go to draw in some external well. You have Jesus in your heart, a fountain springing up to everlasting life.

O soul, how rich thou art, who, passing through Jordan hast come into the good land of rest!

Deliverance from the Power of Sin

PHILIPPIANS 2:12, 13: "Work out your own salvation with fear and trembling. For it is God which worketh in you both to will and to do of His good pleasure."

Salvation. "Work out your own salvation." There is a sense in which salvation is finished. There is another sense in which it is in process. Finished by Christ when He died, and yet in process by the Holy Ghost in our heart.

Salvation is a great prize, with two termini. The first terminus is on the cross, where Jesus saved from the guilt, the penalty of sin; the second terminus is in His second Advent, when the body will be raised and married to the spirit, and salvation will be complete. But between His cross where Jesus put away guilt, and the second Advent where the body is married to the spirit, between these two there is the process of being saved from the power and the love of sin.

In Acts 2:47, and I Corinthians 1:18, the Revised Version in each case speaks of people being saved. "The Lord added to them day by day those that were being saved." "The word of the cross is to them that are perishing, foolishness: but unto us which are being saved it is the power of God."

A man says to me, "Are you saved?"

I reply, "I *was* saved when I trusted Christ; I *shall be* saved when my body is raised; but I am *being saved* all the time." Aye, we are being saved.

Remember that *sin is a parasite*. Your little babe has got measles, scarlatina, scarlet fever; but measles, scarlatina, scarlet fever are not native to it—they are parasites; and it is possible that in a few days they will pass, and your child's skin will be better. So sin is not necessary to human nature. Adam was created without it. Christ, a man, lived without it, and we men and women some day will have got over our mumps and measles and bronchitis, and we shall be whole.

Sin is a parasite. Thank God, the day will come when I shall stand up before my God without a stick or stone of sin. I may carry some scar that sin has left, but sin itself will be gone forever.

NEXT: *God comes into your heart to take your side against the parasite sin.*

A dear friend of mine told me that her boy came back from school with scarlet fever. He came home in a carriage, wrapped in blankets. As he was brought into the hall, she met him and said, "My boy, mother has got a room upstairs for you and herself, and mother is going to sit down by your bed, and she is never going to leave it till you are well, and mother is going to help you fight against the fever."

And she shut herself up in the bed-room with him. Do you think she loved the boy less because he was so long getting well? Once he said to her, "Mother, you have not kissed me lately. Don't you love me quite so much because I have got all these marks?

She kissed him, and said, "I loved you before, but I think I love you better now."

So, dear soul, cursed with the sin which thou hast taken into thy heart, God hates the sin, but He loves thee! He knew all about it before He chose thee. He will never be surprised. He will never be disappointed. He will never love you less. But the more sinful you are, the weaker you are, the more often you have a relapse and go back, the more often you fall, the mother in God—for there is mother as well as father in God—the mother in God who has come into your heart will fight sin step by step with you. Your weakness will command His strongest love.

He sits down beside you. The fever is on your head and body. He knows it will take a long vigil, long care, long patience. He has counted the cost, He is prepared for a long sickness. He has taken you in hand, your passions, your impurity, your garrulous gossip, your sulkiness, your jealousy, your vainglory, your love of money, your love of sin; God knows it all. But He has come, and will never leave you for a moment. If you will let Him, He will make short work. If you resist Him, you will make the work longer. But He will never leave you, He will never give you up, and however often you fall, go back to Him again.

Suppose some mother had a boy with scarlet fever, and in the fever he got delirious, and instead of keeping in bed he kept getting out; it would be very trying, very disappointing. He would throw his recovery back, but the mother would still cling to him. She would be sorry, and disappointed, and wish he had not done it; but she would love him, she could not give the boy up, she would bring him through.

O soul, thou hast thought ill of thy God! Thou hast thought because thou didst so often fall that God was tired of thee. Ah! thou knowest not that His tender mercy is infinite, and He will never let you go, NEVER, until in heaven He kisses your face, out of which the fever and the brand of sin have gone forever. O, my God, thou wilt kiss my soul into health!

Remember further that *His purpose is to deliver from the power of sin.* The *guilt* is gone, but the *power* remains, and He can only deliver from this gradually. Now, understand me. People ask if I believe in progressive or instantaneous sanctification. I reply—first, I do not believe in sanctification, I believe in the Sanctifier; I do not believe in holiness, I believe in the Holy One. Not an *it,* but *a person;* not an attribute, but Christ in my heart. *Instantaneous?* Yes, in this way: that in a moment I can take up the true attitude toward Christ: but *progressive,* because stage after stage He will carry on His work within me, weaning me, saving me from the love and the power of sin, deeper, deeper, deeper down into my heart. I take up the position suddenly, but I apply the position all along my life.

Is not this true? To-day you see things to be wrong which five years ago you permitted, and five years from today you will see things wrong, which you now permit. Evidently the work is progressive. God sheds light upon our life. It is but the twilight at first. In the twilight I can see a chair and a table and a piano and a chiffonier: that is all. But the twilight merges into morning, and in the morning light I can see smaller things: the ornaments, the pictures that are on the wall. But morning becomes noon, and now I see the dust which has gathered. I could not see that in the twilight, but I see it at noon.

So God deals with you and me. He does not turn the heart upside down, and empty it of every sin at once. First the twilight, and we put away obvious sin; then morning, and we put away other sins not seen before; then eleven o'clock in the morning, and we put away deeper sins that we had missed; until it comes toward meridian, and in the perfect light we put away more sins, the small dust we had missed. We see deeper, deeper down, and every year a man is saved more completely from the power of known sin. So it is gradual.

I think it is perfectly absurd for a man to say he is perfectly sanctified. He is not within a thousand miles of it. Once, when in Leicester, I was paying parochial calls, and dropped in on a washerwoman who had just got out a line of clothes. I congratulated my friend because they looked so white. So, very much encouraged by her pastor's kind words, she asked him to have a cup of tea, and we sat down. While we were taking the tea, the sky clouded and there was a snow-storm; and as I came out the white snow lay everywhere, and I said to her, "Your washing does not look quite so clean as it did."

"Ah," she said, "the washing is white enough; but what can stand against God Almighty's white?"

So you may think that you are clean, because you have never seen God. When you see God, your holiest day will seem to be imperfect; you will abhor yourself and repent in dust and ashes, and you will need to say, "Forgive me my debts as I forgive my debtors."

SALVATION FROM KNOWN SIN—BUT NOT FROM TEMPTATION

Still, up to the limit of our light God can keep us from known sin. I will say that again: up to the limit of our light—twilight, morning, noon—up to the limit of our light God is able to keep us from all conscious and known sin. But He will not keep us from temptation. You cannot help the devil knocking at the door, but you can help inviting him in to supper. You cannot help the foul vulture flying over your head, but you can help letting him make a nest in your hair.

When you live near God you will be most tempted of the devil. Some men seem to think they are not holy because they are tempted. I should not believe in a man's holiness if he were not tempted. When I was at school, the boys used to avoid certain orchards, because they were full of crab apples; and you might know that the apples in those orchards were sour, or the boys would go for them. And if you are not tempted, it shows that your heart is empty and wicked, and

NOT WORTH THE DEVIL'S WHILE

to spend his time over. When the Spirit of God descended upon Christ He was led by the Spirit into the wilderness to be tempted of the devil—Spirit-filled, devil-tempted.

You ask, Why does God let us be tempted? I think it is to show where we are weak; that upon the temptation, as our stepping stone, we may reach out for some of

God's help. I would not know how much I needed Christ unless the devil were constantly tempting me.

God is working in you. The compunction you feel when you sin, the yearning you feel for a better life, your desire to go to a religious meeting, all are proofs that God is working in you to deliver you. Many a woman of fashion or society is, perhaps, living in the very whirl of it, and yet, poor thing, in it she really wants something better. My sister, do not be disheartened—that is God working in you! I believe you are a real child of His, but you are so weak, and you do not like to stand alone, you do what other women do, and yet you hate it all the time, and you want the better life. Understand that God is working in you; you are the workshop of God.

WORK OUT WHAT GOD WORKS IN.

Now, I come to my next point. When God works in, you must work out. *"Work out* your own salvation with fear and trembling, for it is GOD that *worketh in* you."

You must work out what God works in, and you must do it with fear and trembling. Let me explain. Suppose a great artist is training a young student. He says to that student, "I am coming into your studio, to help you to-morrow from nine till twelve."

It is a wonderful thing that this illustrious artist should spend three hours with that obscure student; and the man fears. He does not fear the teacher, but he fears lest he will miss a minute of the teacher's help. He trembles, not because he dreads the teacher, but because he is a miser to use up every hint, every suggestion, every touch. O! he trembles lest he should lose anything. So, dear soul, listen. The great God has come into your life to live there, and He says to you, "I am going to save you from the power of sin."

How careful you ought to be! When God speaks, obey. When God gives a hint, instantly act upon it. Be very fearful lest by any word or act of yours, you spoil and thwart and put back God's work in your life. Work out with fear and trembling.

God in you will work to will, and then God in you will work to do what He wills. First, God works to will. He does not work to make you feel, because feeling ends in smoke so often. God does not work in you to think, because you think and think again. But God works in you to *will*. That is, there rises up in your heart a *desire* which becomes at last a *purpose* to be free. No one knows it, no one guesses it; but in your soul there rises up the will.

God is always definite. The devil confounds us by bringing a number of points before us, but when God deals with us He deals with one point at a time. He takes one sin, one failure, one incumbrance or weight. When you are at the communion table, when you are alone, when you are reading your Bible, this one thing comes up. God works away there. Now meet Him there, and He will work in you to will against it. That is the first thing. That was so with me.

About seventeen years ago, when God began to work with me, there was a thing in my life no one knew; but in my silent hour God worked in me to will that it should cease. I was so weak I could not put it away.

Blessed be God, the willing and the doing are from Him, and by faith you look to Him to do for you what you cannot do for yourself.

I have found God works thus. He leads me to see a thing to be wrong, and then I put my will against it. Whenever it comes towards me, God says, "It is coming. Hide, hide in the cleft of the Rock. I see it coming."

It is like a chick—a hawk—the mother; I run—I hide—the devil finds me in Christ. And if I fall through not trusting Him to keep me, He works in me to be sorry, and I am sorry; and then He works in me to confess.

Two years ago, one Sunday morning, on coming down to my church, I found that the verger had done a very foolish thing, for vergers (though they live in the church) are not immaculate. I lost my temper. I was going to preach within a quarter of an hour. As a result of losing my temper, I was as far out of fellowship with God as a man may get. My officers were all coming in to pray with me before I entered the pulpit. I did not know what to do. I knew I had fallen. I knew I dared not preach God's gospel until I was right with man, because one cannot be more right with God than with his brother man; one's position as a man is the gauge and indicator of one's position before God. I thought they would all think that I was crazy, but I rang the bell, called the verger in, and said to him, "You did an uncommonly unwise thing just now—I cannot take that back: but that did not exonerate me for losing my temper. Forgive me."

The man looked more startled than pleased, but that did not matter. I had done what was right, and my soul shot into the blue of God's heaven again. God worked in me to confess.

A man loses his temper with his wife at breakfast. He goes downtown. All the morning he wishes that he had not done it, and the Spirit of God in him says, "Tell her when you get home that you are sorry."

No, we men are very tough material, and instead he says, "I will buy her a basket of strawberries."

He comes with his little peace-offering. She, poor dear, understands it. She has lived long enough to know that he is only mortal, and she takes the offering as an apology. But he would have been a manlier and a happier and a more Christlike man if he had said, "Wife, I am a minister, I am an elder, I am a good man really, but I was away from God, and the devil tripped me up. Forgive me, sweetheart, forgive me."

That would be the best way. And when God works in you to confess, confess! Confess to man, to woman, to child, to servant, to Him; and His blood will wash you whiter than snow.

How long does it take between confession and forgiveness? When I was a boy at school and talked to the boy next to me, they sent me down to the bottom of the class, and it took me a month to work up. When you do wrong and confess it, God does not put you down and leave you to work up for a whole month, but on the spot, immediately, He forgives you and restores your soul, and puts you back where you were before you fell.

Only, dear soul, abide in Jesus. Let the Holy Ghost in you keep you abiding in Jesus, so that when Satan comes to knock at your door, Jesus will go and open it, and as soon as the devil sees the face of Christ looking through the door, he will turn tail like a whipped cur. Let Jesus live in your heart. Do you live in Jesus? When the devil comes, do not meet him yourself, but let Jesus meet him, and you stand behind Him. The Negro said:

"When the devil comes to me, I always introduce him to his betters." Put Jesus between you and the devil. Live in Christ. God will work in you. He will make you hate sin. He will make you loathe what you loved. He will deliver you deeper, ever deeper in your life, from the power and the love of sin. It may be a long process before the work is done, but He will keep you from known sin, and save you ever deeper down in your heart.

Oh, Thou who art able to keep us from stumbling and to present us faultless before Thy glory with exceeding joy, to Thee, Emmanuel, Christ, Son of God, lover of my soul, I yield my life, my soul, my all!

God's Two Men

IN THE SIGHT OF GOD there are two men. "The first man Adam was made a living soul; the last Adam was made a life-giving Spirit. The first man is of the earth, earthy; the second man is the Lord from heaven." I Corinthians 15:45, 47.

I want to speak now about these two men.

The first man. God took the red clay and molded a man in His own image. See! that man is taking his nature out of the hand of God, so that instead of God being its center, he becomes his own center as he takes the forbidden fruit. Next, he is expelled, and in his expulsion from Paradise the whole race passes out. A legend states that as he and Eve passed out, Eve plucked a flower to take with her, but it withered as she passed the gate. At that moment you and I and all our race passed out of Paradise. Three things followed: the bead-drop of sweat upon the brow; the pang of travail for the woman; and death. The sweat of toil for man, pain through which all the children of life are born, and the earth seamed with graves. Finally Adam begets a son in his own image; that is, every child born outside the gate of Paradise has a bias to keep outside, no bias to go back. And just as in England, when a man plays bowls upon the sward, each bowl leaving the hand has a bias to turn off the straight, so every one of us is born with a bias off the right. By our first birth we all inherit a lost Paradise, sweat, travail, death, and bias to evil.

Now the second man. I see Him first driven by the gust of temptation as He too stands before the element of life. The first Adam was tempted by a tree, the second Adam was tempted by bread. Just as the first Adam made self and passion his rule, the second Adam made the will of God His rule and said, "If God says I'm not to eat, I'll not eat. Man shall not live by bread only, but by the Word of God," So Milton was perfectly right when he made "Paradise Regained" turn upon Christ's victory over temptation.

See that second man. The bead-drop stands upon His brow also, for He sits by the well at Sychar, tired. The pang of travail is in His heart, too, for He bears the infirmity of man, and by His travail a new earth and a new heaven are born. He also tastes death, He dies. So that there is nothing in our lot as man, except the bias to sin, that He does not know.

Look on yonder cross! The second man is dying. In yonder grave He lies, but from that grave He breaks and is the first man to rise. You remind me of Lazarus. But he did not enter into resurrection; he was simply a prisoner on parole, who went back to death again. But this Man in death and through death passed into resurrection; and if you want to know what you and your dear ones will some day be, study the risen Christ. He spoke, and Mary recognized His voice; and our dear ones will speak to us one day, and we shall recognize their voices. He spoke about the things which had happened on the other side of His death; and our dear ones will talk with us some day about the scenes of Bethany and Nazareth and Galilee where they and we walked oft together.

But mark the risen Man. He passes to the ascension mountain. I never can understand why the Church has made so little of the resurrection and ascension, the ascension pre-eminently. On the ascension mountain He says farewell. In the early morning He had left the city. I suppose the disciples followed Him; they saw Him, but nobody else. The people who met them going through the street saw disciples, but they did not see the risen Saviour who preceded them. They came together to the ascension mountain, and He blessed them, and began to ascend, and a cloud, like a chariot sent from His Father's home to fetch Him back, received Him.

Ephesians 1:21 tells us what happened on the other side of the cloud. We are told that "principalities, and powers, and might, and dominion, and every name that is named, not only in this world, but also in that which is to come"—all waited there to contest our Saviour's path. Ephesians 6:12 shows that these principalities and powers were not bright angels, but devils from hell: "We wrestle not against flesh and blood, but against principalities, against powers, against the rulers of the darkness of the world, against spiritual wickedness in high places." All hell was there that morning, sworn to stop Christ from going back. Why? If Christ had been content to go back as *God,* the devil would have been too sensible to stop Him, for God must go back to God. But Christ took man in Him. He was *man,* the glorified, risen, ascending man, the second Adam; and all hell tried to stop Christ taking the man to the throne of God.

He may go as God, but He must not go as the representative man; or else, just as in the first man the race came out of Paradise, so, in the second man, all who believe in Him will re-enter Paradise. Therefore the devil must stop it if he can. But you might as well try to stop a cork rising by piling sea-water on it, as try to stop Christ's rising by piling devils on Him. He went through them, and passed into the heavens; and for the first time—and it is so wonderful!—for the first time in the history of the universe the creature was taken into union with the eternal God at the very throne of God Himself.

Now, friends, understand that your nature as a man is the regnant nature, the ruling nature in the universe. In the universe our human nature is

THE SUPREME CREATED POWER.

O wonderful nature which I possess, and which is worn by the Son of Man, so that dying Stephen said, "I see the heavens opened, and the Son of Man standing at the right hand of God"!

I stop for a moment, and I call upon every one to raise his heart and say, "Worthy art Thou, O Son of Man who art also Son of God!" Crowns, crowns, crowns for the exalted second man!

Now remember, by the first birth we are all in the first man, and by the second birth we may all be in the second man. You are born by nature into Adam the first, you are born by grace into Adam the second. "As many as received Him, to them gave He the right to become the sons of God, even to them that believe on His name."

Thank God, you may be born again as you sit listening to my voice! Look at my hand. That hand has two sides, the one toward the ceiling, the other toward this floor; two sides of the same hand. That hand shall stand for the act by which we become united with Christ. That act has two sides. Angels in heaven call it "being born again"; men on earth call it "trusting in Jesus." If you trust Jesus you are born again, and if you are born again you will trust Jesus, and you cannot tell which comes first, any more than you can tell which spoke of the wheel begins to move first. They all move together.

Now, soul, listen. In the past you have been a gay and frivolous woman, or you have been a money-loving man. You have lived a butterfly life, and you have come to hear me, you hardly know why. Someone asked you, and you thought you might pass an hour or two. I tell you that if you will unite yourself with Jesus Christ who died for us, if you will lift your heart to Him now and say, "Jesus, I come to Thee, and trust Thee as my Saviour," you may not have tears or emotion or a paroxysm, or feel at all, but you do it in cold blood, you do it by an act of your will, you choose Christ. The moment you do that, the Holy Spirit of God binds you in a living union with Christ, and the germ of a new life is put into your soul. You are *born again!* It will begin to work. It may take years before it works out; but it will begin to work instantaneously, and you will belong to the aristocracy of the universe, Jesus Christ and the new humanity.

Now we must go a step further. It is one of the most wonderful things in the Bible to discover what is known as the aorist tense, the Greek aorist, the definite past act. Now that aorist is used in Ephesians 2:5, 6, where the Apostle says, as in Colossians, that we were quickened with Christ, were raised with Christ, ascended with Christ, and are seated at the right hand of God.

Now follow me. God knew all those who would believe in Jesus and become united with Him, and Jesus stood for all of them. When He was on the cross, all who were to believe, who shall believe, His one true Church—all were on the cross in Him, and in Christ we paid the penalty of our sins. It is impossible for me to go to hell, because God saw to it that my sin was punished when I died in Christ. I paid my debt when I died nearly nineteen hundred years ago in God's purpose in Christ. Then when He lay in the grave, and women and men bore Him there and put Him to what appeared to be His last sleep, you and I and all the church lay in the grave too.

My brother, if you go back and live a worldly life, you have to go back through the grave to it, because the grave lies between the body of Christ, of which you are a part, and the world that cast Him out. The world cast Him out, and when they cast Him out they cast us out also, and we were buried in Christ by the world that hates the church.

But just as Eve was taken out of Adam as he slept, the Church was taken out of Christ in His sleep, and when He rose we streamed out a great procession from the grave. And on Easter morning I celebrate not only the resurrection of Christ but my own, for I too was raised in Him.

Oh! it was a good thing when, as I crossed the Atlantic, we got through that storm. It was such a storm that I could hardly preach to the people in the saloon, the ship was rocking so; but after a while we got through the disturbance, and left the storm behind us. And in

Christ, when He died, the ark of God carried you and me through the storm of death into clear water, and above us is the blue sky of God's love.

On ascension day I celebrate my ascension also, and in God's purpose all of us who believe are seated in Christ, and we must live day by day as those who in God's purpose have passed into the heavenly life.

You tell me that when I die my eternity will begin. No such thing. My eternity began when I was born in Christ. Eternal life is in my heart to-day, and the only difference that will come to me when I pass through what men call death, but which to me is not death—it is only the shadow of death, for I died in Christ, and I can never pass again through the agony of death, but I will pass through the shadow of death, and no one was ever hurt by a shadow yet, although they may have been a little fearful—the only difference that will come to me is that I shall get rid, for a time at least, of a rather crazy body, which will lie to wait until my spirit rejoins it in perfect beauty. But God will never love me more than He does to-day, and I shall never be nearer God than I am to-day and already I hunger no more, nor thirst any more, neither does the sun smite me nor any heat, because already the Lamb is leading me day by day to living fountains of waters, and God is wiping all tears from my eyes. Eternity is begun.

Now let us see just how this works out.

POSITION

First, as to your position before God. Your position is IN CHRIST. You are standing to-day in Christ. Never forget to distinguish between your standing and your experience. Your *standing* is in Christ, your *experience* is in your emotion. John Bunyan says that our emotion is like our spending money, the money we have in our pocket: it is sometimes more, but generally less; but our standing in our Forerunner is like the money we have in the bank, which is not affected by our daily expenses. I am sometimes happy, sometimes worn, over-tired, inclined to be nervous; but I never mind, because it does not matter to me whether I pass through the dark and the valley of sorrow and all transient depression. My position is unaffected because it is settled in my Forerunner, my Priest, my Saviour, my Head, in whom I stand before God. Oh, blessed be God for that! Do not look, therefore, for evidence in your emotions, but look for your title deeds in Christ the Forerunner.

VICTORY

Next, look at your victory. In Christ you are above the devil. Now mark: The devil was made to be God's vice-gerent. He fell. In his stead God made man to have dominion over the earth, and the devil swore that man should never be superior to him. He thought he could get man down under his feet, so he breathed hell into man, and men fell into selfishness, which is hell; and the devil laughed:

"Ha, ha, I am supreme!"

Moses went under, Job went under, David went under, all men went under the devil. But Christ came, a man, and the devil fell beneath Him thrice; three galling throws in the wilderness. All through Christ's life He cast the legions out. The devil came to Him on the cross, and Christ broke his head. The devil came to Him in the ascension, and Christ trod upon him. And in Christ our Head, our humanity, our manhood, our new race trod the devil under, and in spite of all that the devil could do, the second Man, the Lord from heaven, took the superior position, and you and I took it too in Him. When, therefore the devil comes to us, let us remind him that he is inferior to Christ. The devil-nature is inferior to the Christ-nature, and if you have got the Christ-nature in you, the devil is inferior to you.

I was once trying to explain this to a man. Said I to him, "To what part of the body of Christ do you belong?"

He said, "I don't know."

"Well," said I, "do you belong to the eye in His mystical body?"

"No," said he, "I don't weep enough."

"Do you belong to His mouth?"

"No, I don't speak enough."

"Do you belong to His heart?"

"No," said he, "I don't love enough."

"Do you belong to His hand?"

"No, sir, I don't do enough."

I said, "Man alive, if you are a Christian, you are in some part of the body of Christ. Where are you?"

"Well," he said, "I may be in His feet."

"Well, if you are in His feet, that will serve my purpose, for it is written, He will put all enemies under His feet."

And so it is proved beyond doubt and forevermore that the man who has got Christ in him is devil-proof. The devil cannot touch him if he abides in Christ.

Now, the only way in which the devil can get the better of you is to strew some crumbs to get you from under the wing of Christ. As long as you stay there, the devil cannot touch you. So he puts some little morsels of worldly pleasure, and evil imagination, and lust, and passion, and he says: "Come along, come along, come along!" and when you come out, he has you. But if you keep in Christ he cannot touch you. Abide in Christ and let Christ abide in you, and the devil has no power.

POSSESSION

One thing more. Ephesians 4:8: "Wherefore he saith, When He ascended up on high He led captivity captive, and gave gifts unto men." Acts 2:33: "Therefore being by the right hand of God exalted, and having received of the Father the promise of the Holy Ghost, He hath shed forth this which ye now see and hear."

When the Son of Man entered the presence of the Father as our forerunner and representative, Peter tells us (the Greek word bears the meaning), that He asked the Father for the Holy Spirit. As the second person in the Holy Trinity, Jesus was one with the Father and the Holy Spirit before all time, but when He became man He put out of use the attributes of His deity for the time being. At any moment He might have used them, and indeed the devil tried to induce Him to do so, but He refused, and was content to live the human life in the power of God received into His human nature. When He went up to God it was still as the ascended, glorified, representative man; and as such He came to His Father and said, so to speak:

"Father, I have glorified Thee on the earth, I have finished the work which Thou gavest Me to do. And now I come to Thee, and behind Me there are millions of spirits that are following on the way that I have made for them, millions who are to believe in Me, to become united with Me by faith, and who soon will come to be with Me where I am. I ask nothing for Myself, it is enough for Me to be with You again; but I ask for them that Thou wouldest give to Me as their representative, the fullness of the Holy Ghost, that what I have had I may be able to communicate to them."

So He received of the Father the promise of the Holy Ghost; not as God, because as such He was one with the Holy Ghost, but as man, as the representative man, that He might be able to communicate Him to men.

A friend of mine was in Switzerland, and two Englishmen came into the hotel where he was staying, and engaged three guides. They were going to take a very precipitous ascent up the side of a mountain, a piece of ice which was almost as steep as the side of a house. When they reached the spot they roped themselves together: a guide, a traveler, a guide, a traveler, a guide. They commenced to climb, and by cutting notches in the ice wall they were able to place the toes of their feet. So they crept up, and they had nearly reached the top, when in some way the last man lost his footing and began to sway. He pulled down the man above him, and he too began to swing slowly to and fro. The two pulled down the third, and the third, the fourth, and all four were swinging over the precipice in imminent danger of being dashed to pieces. The only thing that kept them was the rope around the waist of the first man. As soon as he felt the strain, he took his ice axe and drove it hard into the ice just above him, and held to it for life; and as he stood for an instant or two, the man next him regained his footing, the man beneath, his, and so on to the end of the line, and the whole five stood because the first man stood.

You understand the application. You and I have no power; we swing to and fro; but by faith we are bound to Christ, and because He is in the glory and stands up there, we shall be pulled up at last from the difficulties of this present life, to stand with Him forever in His Father's presence.

The Anointing with the Holy Spirit

THERE IS NO NEED for me to prove or attempt to prove that the Holy Ghost is a person. In the Greek, though the name for the Holy Ghost is neuter, it is followed by a personal pronoun *autos,* which could not be used unless the Holy Spirit was a person. Readers of the English Bible will remember that the Holy Spirit said, "Separate me Barnabas and Saul," and the Apostle says, "Grieve not the Holy Spirit." Only a person can designate workmen, and only a person with tender nature could be grieved. As you worship the Father and the Son, worship the Holy Spirit; three persons, but one God.

Before Pentecost the Holy Spirit brooded over our world. In chaos He moved to educe cosmos. He wrought in holy men to inspire the Word of God. He prepared the way for Christ. But Pentecost was His birthday. Just as Jesus Christ was in the world before His incarnation, but His incarnation was His birthday into the body, so the Holy Ghost was in the world before Pentecost, but on the day of Pentecost He was born into the body of Christ. And as the body born of the virgin was the home of Christ, and through it He wrought, so the Church is the body of the Holy Spirit, through which He is working during this era, until the body shall rejoin the

Head, and Head and body make one entity, a new man forevermore. As the manger was the cradle of Christ, so the upper chamber in Jerusalem was the cradle of the Holy Spirit's incarnation. Hence the Roman Catholic Church, claiming that she is the only true church, calls herself the see of the Holy Ghost. The word "see" is the Latin *sedes,* a seat. The Church of Rome says she is the seat of the Holy Ghost, and thus takes to herself that which is the province of the Holy Catholic Church; the body of Christ, which is not visible, but which consists of all who believe, is the seat, the see, the throne, of the most Holy Spirit.

Men talk as though God were an absentee. But every true believer, every audience gathered in the name of Christ, is the home, the see, the body of God the Holy Spirit.

Now on the day of Pentecost the Holy Spirit came to give power to the preaching of the gospel. Jesus Christ was conceived of the Holy Ghost. The Holy Thing born of the pure virgin was wrought by the Holy Spirit, and through thirty years Jesus was led and taught amid His native hills by the divine Spirit. Beneath His impulse our Lord went down to the Jordan, and being baptized He identified Himself with the sins of men: for the Jordan was (so to speak) saturated with the sin that was confessed over it, and when Jesus Christ stepped into it He became (as it were) identified with the sin of the race, though He Himself was sinless. From the Jordan He went forth to His work, but not before the sky had been rift, and the Holy Spirit had come upon Him with the gentle movement of a dove.

What! had He not been conceived by the Holy Spirit? Yes. Was He not one with the Holy Spirit? Certainly. Why then should He be again anointed? Because His human nature needed to be empowered by the Holy Spirit before even He could do successful service in the world. Jesus waited for thirty years until He was anointed, and only then did He say, "The Spirit of the Lord God is upon me, (Greek *epi,* UPON me), and He hath anointed me to preach."

How absurd it is for us to send young men to college to equip them with intellectual store of classic and philosophic learning, and to send them out to teach, without insisting upon it that if Christ waited to be anointed before He went to preach, no young man ought to preach until he, too, has been anointed of the Holy Ghost!

For three years our Lord wrought in the power of the Holy Ghost. Never forget that our Lord's ministry was not in the power of the second person of the Holy Trinity, but in the power of the third person of the Holy Trinity. As Saint Peter said, "God anointed Him with the Holy Ghost, and He went about doing good." On the cross He offered Himself to God in the power of the eternal Spirit. He was raised from the dead by the Holy Ghost, and during the forty days He gave command to His apostles in and by the Holy Ghost. And before He went, He said to His disciples that as He received His Pentecost at the Jordan, He would see that the Church had her Pentecost too. He was conceived of the Holy Ghost, but He was anointed by the Holy Ghost. The Church was conceived by the Holy Ghost, but the Church, before attempting her ministry, must also be anointed by the Holy Ghost; and what the baptism in Jordan was to the Head, the day of Pentecost was to the Body.

The Head communicated the Holy Ghost to the body, as I explained in the preceding address.

I ask every Bible student to note that wonderful word: "He *received* of the Father the promise of the Holy Ghost." No sooner had He received it than He turned to see if His people were prepared to receive it, and then He opened the window of heaven and poured down a Niagara upon His Church; and ever since He has been there in the glory, charged, yes, charged with the power of the Holy Spirit. And just as a man may touch a man charged with electricity and a spark will answer, so you cannot touch the living Christ by faith without the spark of the Holy Ghost flashing into your soul.

Brethren, the Greek preposition *epi* is significant of Pentecost. Pentecost differs from regeneration. In regeneration the Holy Spirit is described as being *within,* but in Pentecost and ever after the Holy Ghost is described as being *upon*. He anoints, He falls upon, He equips; and I ask that before this meeting shall close, everyone in this audience who has been regenerated by the Holy Ghost shall become anointed, filled, empowered with the Holy Ghost. It would make

THE GREATEST DIFFERENCE POSSIBLE IN YOUR LIFE.

There is where you have failed, my brother. You have been preaching the cross, but you have not been preaching the cross in the demonstration and power of the blessed Spirit.

When I was at Leicester, there were many discharged

prisoners whom I took from the prison gate to my house, where they lived with me, under my care. I had a firewood factory. The great beams came from Norway, and they were sawed up by a circular saw wrought by a crank, and on that crank fifteen men were kept at work to give them an opportunity of regaining their character. But these men served me ill. I lost much money. I presently swept them away, and instead purchased a gas-engine, and the gas-engine did in an hour as much work as the fifteen discharged prisoners did in eight hours.

One day I asked my circular saw how it was that it turned out so much work, and the saw at first said it could not tell. I asked if it had been sharpened. It said no. I asked if it had been polished. It said no. I asked if it had been oiled. It said no. Then I said:

"How is it?"

"Why," it replied, "I think there is a stronger driving power behind me. Something is working through me with a new force. It is not I, it is the power behind."

Would God that you, my brother ministers, who have been working with the power of intellect, of energy, of enthusiastic zeal, with but poor effect, may become linked to the power of God the Holy Ghost stored in Christ; for as soon as you shall link to it, not you, but the power of God through you, will repeat the marvels of Pentecost.

One word more here. You ask me if the day of Pentecost was a specimen day. I answer: yes, and for two reasons. First, on the day of Pentecost the priest in the Temple presented twelve loaves, the specimen and the result of the harvest; and inasmuch as God chose the day of Pentecost for the outpouring of the Holy Spirit, He surely meant us to understand that the day of Pentecost was a specimen day, and that what He did that day He was prepared to do every day; and He would have done it if the church had not choked and frustrated His plans. Secondly, in Acts 2:39 you have these words of Peter, "This promise is unto you, and to your children, and to all that are afar off, even as many as the Lord our God shall call." Understand therefore that the promise of Pentecost is for you also, because God has called you, and from to-day you may go forth charged with power from on high.

HOW MAY WE GET THIS ANOINTING?

Now a step further. You say to me, "Sir, tell me how I may get this power myself."

I will. I know a little of it, thank God, and I hope as the years pass that I may know more and more. This truth has revolutionized my life.

Any mechanic knows this law to be true: obey the law of a force, and the force will obey you. I repeat it: obey the law of a force, and that force will obey you. Take water-force. I cannot make water do my will until I understand the law upon which it works. If I want water to go up hill, I must study the law by which water seeks its own level; and if I construct my machinery to obey the law of falling water, then having obeyed the law of water, water will obey me. What has Edison been doing for the last twenty years in his laboratory? He has been studying the law of electricity, and having studied the law upon which electricity works, he has constructed his machinery to obey that law; and ever since he perfected his obedience, electricity has been his slave, and there is nothing he cannot make electricity perform if only he is patient and wise enough to understand the method on which electricity will work.

I once asked some men this very profound question, "When was there more electricity in the world—now, or away back a hundred years?"

They all said there was more electricity in the world to-day than there had ever been before. Poor fools they must have been to come to such a conclusion. Why, before Adam stepped the sward of Paradise there was as much electricity in the cloud, in the air, and in nature as there is to-day, only man did not understand the law of electricity, and therefore electricity would not obey his summons. There was plenty of electricity, but men never used it.

So is it with the Holy Spirit. There is as much Holy Spirit power in your little village church, my brother, as there is in the large tabernacle in the country, and the mistake of your life has been that you have never yet learned the law of the Holy Ghost; for if you had, the Holy Ghost would have come flowing through your life as much as through the life of a Peter or a John. You seem to think that God is a God of favoritism. You seem to think that God has His chosen favorites whom He endues with the Holy Ghost here and there, while all the rest are left to take their chance. I admit that the gifts of the living Christ are given on His sovereign decision, but the power of the Holy Ghost is FOR EVERYONE, for you.

Now let me tell you briefly the conditions on which, if you obey them, you may at this moment and from now be able to—I was going to say, but perhaps it is too startling,—to *command* the Holy Ghost. I think I will say that, however, because God says, "Of the work of My hand command ye Me." And if a man will obey God to the uttermost, he may command the power of God at any moment.

Now what are these conditions? They are as far as I know five. If you discover another, let me know.

FIVE CONDITIONS

First. *You cannot have the power of the Holy Ghost without having the Holy Ghost Himself.*

That is, the Holy Ghost must come to you as a person before you can enjoy His attribute. In other words, you must be a holy man before you can wield the power of the Holy Ghost. There are plenty of men who think that if they could only get the power of the Holy Ghost they would be able to fill their churches and sell their books and get themselves name and fame. They want *it,* but not *Him.* You cannot have it without having Him. If you want the power of the Holy Ghost, open your heart to-day and be filled with the Holy Ghost, and then you will have His power.

Second. *You must be cleansed.*

Oh, I do not want to speak wisely! I do not want needlessly to offend you, or denounce you. But I do feel in my heart that if the Holy Spirit is going to work through you or anybody He must have a cleansed vessel. The body must be clean.

Now I know that I might here dilate on many of those indulgences that men and women permit. I would much prefer not to characterize them, because you yourselves know anything in your life which is inconsistent with the perfect majesty and purity of that Spirit who has made your body His temple. But if my body is really the temple, the residence and the throne of the Holy Ghost, I must be as careful of it as I would be if I were the custodian of a temple in the inner part of which the light of God shone. I need not say more than that.

Third. *You must live for the glory of Christ as your supreme end.*

Jesus Christ came into the world to glorify the Father, and the Holy Ghost came into the world to glorify the Son. If therefore you want the Holy Ghost to work with you, you must agree with the Holy Ghost to glorify Jesus, for the Spirit was not given till Jesus was glorified.

Fourth. *Your preaching and teaching must be in harmony with the Word of God.*

I am a Quaker by extraction, and I glory in it, especially when I know what they have been in this country. I dissent from them because I believe they went wrong when they magnified the Holy Spirit to the exclusion, in many cases, of the Word of God. And with all love I would say that if there is one danger ahead for the Salvation Army of the present day, it is lest they should magnify the work of the Spirit of God in experience, apart from the Word of God taught to their converts. Remember that the Holy Spirit is like a locomotive, the Word of God like the steel rails; and you must have the steel rails of the Bible as well as the steam-power of the Holy Ghost. Let the Holy Ghost fill you, but He will work along that Book. And I hold that the fact that the Holy Spirit elects to work through that Book is its most complete vindication against all that modern critics have to say. As long as the Holy Ghost is prepared to stand by it and to work by it, I hold it to be in an incomparable sense the Word of the living God to man. I am well satisfied to accept it all, Jonah and the fish included.

Fifth, and last. *The Holy Spirit must be received by faith.* Galatians 3:14 is the battle-axe. I would not be without that text for anything: "That we might receive the promise of the Spirit through faith."

All God's dealings with men are on the same principle, by faith. By faith you are regenerate, by faith you are justified, by faith you are sanctified, by faith you receive the Holy Ghost, by faith you receive Christ as the power of God into your life. It is all by faith.

Let me close with this bit of personal experience. I have always gone on the principle that our moral constitution is on the same plan; that just as our faces are made on the same plan, so our moral nature is made on the same plan; and one of the keynotes of my life has been: Understand yourself, and you will understand something of everybody else.

I had been for a long time a minister in Leicester, with a large church and of considerable influence in the city, but very unhappy. Conscious that I had not received the power of the Holy Ghost, I went up to that little village, the name of which you hear so often, Keswick. A great number of God's people gathered there to seek and to receive the power of the Holy Spirit, and they elected to have a prayer-meeting from nine o'clock to eleven and onwards, to pray for the Holy Ghost. A great many people were there agonizing. I was too tired to agonize, and I somehow felt that God did not want me to agonize hour after hour, but I had to learn to *take;* that God wanted to give, and I had only to take.

To-morrow your little girl will come down to breakfast. She is very hungry, and the bread and milk or the oatmeal is on the table. You do not say, "Little girlie, run upstairs, and agonize, roll on the floor for an hour, and then come down."

You say to her, "Little one, I am so glad you have got a good appetite. Now there is your chair, in you get, say your prayer, and start away."

That is what God says to the soul. Those all-nights of prayer for the Holy Ghost are principally necessary to get the people who pray into a fit condition to receive the Holy Ghost; for when the people are ready the Holy Ghost will come without agonizing.

So I left that prayer-meeting at Keswick. It was eleven o'clock or half past eleven, and I crept out into the lane and away from the little village. The lights died away in the distance, and stood on the hill, or walked to and fro, the stars shining upon me, and now and again a little cloud dropping a baptism of rain upon my face, as though symbolic of the refreshing my soul was to receive. As I walked I said, "Oh, my God, if there is a man in this village who needs the power of the Holy Ghost to rest upon him it is I; but I do not know how to receive Him. I am too tired, too worn, too nervously down to agonize."

A voice said to me, "As you took forgiveness from the hand of the dying Christ, take the Holy Ghost from the hand of the living Christ."

I turned to Christ and said, "Lord, as I breathe in this

whiff of warm night air, so I breathe into every part of me Thy blessed Spirit."

I felt no hand laid upon my head, there was no lambent flame, there was no rushing sound from heaven; but by faith, without emotion, without excitement I took, and took for the first time, and I have kept on taking ever since.

I turned to leave the mountainside, and as I went down, the tempter said, "You have got nothing. It is moonshine."

I said, "I have."

He said, "Do you feel it?"

"I do not."

"Then if you do not feel it you have not got it."

I said, "I do not feel it, but I reckon that God is faithful, and He could not have brought a hungry soul to claim by faith, and then give a stone for bread, and a scorpion for a fish. I know I have got it because God led me to claim."

I met a number of young clergymen, and they fought it with me. They said, "No, no, we feel, we feel to have it, and we know we have got it."

But said I to them, "How will you do to-morrow morning when you do not feel it? Now I, who take by faith, am independent of feeling to-morrow or any future time."

While we were talking a young merchant who was listening said, "I want to say a word. You parsons have been talking a great deal about the Holy Spirit. Now I know I have received the Holy Spirit when I have most of Jesus, and in my place at Glasgow, if I miss the presence of Jesus for half an hour, I go into my counting-house, and kneel down and say, 'Holy Spirit, what have I done to Thee that Thou hast taken from me the sense of the presence of Christ?' "

"Oh," we said, "when we know we have most of Christ, when we love Him most, live for Him most, we know that the Holy Ghost is within us in power."

So, brothers, sisters, may I ask you to let this day be the time of transaction with God. Walk to and fro, and say if you like, "I sadly need a Pentecost. As far as I know, I fulfill the conditions, in my will at least."

Then put your hand upon your heart, and say, "I do now receive."

Let the devil say what he likes. Keep reckoning that the Spirit of Christ rests upon you, and when you come to your Jordan, and the students are there to look on, and you might draw back—that Jordan representing your temptation, your mission, some bit of work to do—say, "Holy Spirit, I now trust Thee to do through me Thy Pentecostal work in glorifying Christ."

The Infilling of the Holy Spirit

WE HAVE FOLLOWED CHRIST in His ascension, as entering the presence of His Father. He asked and received from God the Holy Spirit. We have also seen how Christ made Christians. "Christ" means "anointed"; "Christian" means "anointed one." The words "chrism" and "Christ" are identical in derivation. A man becomes truly a Christian when he is anointed with the Holy Spirit.

I speak now of the other aspect of Pentecost, because, though it is quite true that Pentecost means *the anointing on the head and heart,* it also means *the infilling of the Holy Spirit.* Therefore, in Acts 2:4 we are told that they were all—women and men, laymen and apostles—all were alike "filled with" the Holy Spirit.

Now, Ephesians 5:18 gives each one of us a positive command: "Be filled with the Spirit." It is very remarkable that in Acts 2 and Ephesians 5 the infilling of the Holy Spirit in its effect is compared to the effects of wine on the physical system. "Be not drunk with wine, wherein is excess, but be filled with the Spirit," and you can never have excess, you can never have too much of the Spirit.

There are three points of comparison that I want you to notice—joy, speech, power.

First. Wine produces a sense of exhilaration. A drunken man will sing as he reels to his home, and when a man is really filled with the Holy Ghost he becomes a singing Christian, and a Spirit-filled church is always a singing church. Every great outburst of the Holy Spirit's power has been accompanied by singing. Luther's revival spread through Germany by singing Luther's hymns. Whitefield was accompanied by a Wesley, and Moody by a Sankey, and in Germany the Moravian Church has given to us the songs of Gerhardt, with many more.

Secondly. A man who is filled with wine is garrulous. He talks: you cannot keep him still. And a man who is filled with the Holy Spirit talks; he cannot keep silence, he must tell what God has done.

Thirdly. A man who is filled with wine is conscious of a great increase of power. He feels as if he could stand alone against the world. So the man who is filled with the Holy Ghost is full also of the power of God.

Now this filling of the Holy Spirit may come suddenly, or more unconsciously, just as in Scotland they have what they call a "spate" of water, or a well may fill up with water percolating in drop by drop. Whenever the spirit of man, smitten with thirst, comes to Christ, and opens its whole content towards Christ, instantly Christ begins to infill that spirit. It may not be conscious of the gradual infilling, but by His grace He will never stay His hand until the earthly system has been filled to the very full from the river of God, which is full of water.

Now there are three tenses used in the Greek of this filling. In Acts 13:52 we are told of the converts in the highlands of Galatia that they *were being filled* with joy and with the Holy Ghost all the time. They were like some mountain tarn which is always being filled from the melting of the snows above; and as the water flows on to enrich the pasture land beneath, so water is ever percolating in from the upper snow. O child of God, be a brimming lakelet or tarn, on the one hand always giving out to a dying world, but always kept full because you receive every moment from Jesus!

Then Acts 6:5 tells us that Stephen was a man *full* of the Holy Ghost—"full," the adjective; from which I gather that he was an equable man. He did not have fits and starts, he was not now lifted up and then depressed; but always, whenever you met Stephen, there was the same heavenly look, the same tender, gracious word, the same perfect beauty of character, and the same eagerness to glorify Christ. Oh, beloved friends, I wish that you may keep on being filled, and that you may always be full!

And then, Acts 4:8 tells us that Peter, though he had been filled on the day of Pentecost, nevertheless was suddenly *filled again* as he had to speak to the Sanhedrin. I suppose that for a moment he centered himself on God; he looked up, and received a sudden and immediate and complete equipment for his work.

Beloved minister, you may be a man full of the Holy Ghost in your family, but when you kneel in your vestry before entering your pulpit, before attempting a mission, before undertaking any definite work for God by lip or pen, be sure that you are specially equipped by a new reception of the Holy Ghost. In my own life I have found it absolutely necessary, after such a mission as this, when the whole system has become exhausted by the demand made upon the spirit, the nerve, and the physical strength, to get quietly away with God, and to renew one's strength by receiving out of the fullness of the Holy Ghost, breathing in a new supply.

Now you will notice also that the work of the Holy Spirit of Pentecost, filling the heart, has

CERTAIN DEFINITE RESULTS

in the character of the believer; and these are set forth by Christ in three verses, each of which begins with the words: "In that day." When the day of Pentecost breaks upon the spirit, it brings with it three distinct things.

In John 14:20 the Lord says, *"In that day* [that day when the light of Pentecost has pierced the windowpane of your heart, and has chased out the darkness, and has filled you within] in that day you shall know three things: (1.) That I am in My Father, in the light of light, in the rare atmosphere of deity, in God. You shall know that I am in the Father, so that you will never be frightened of the Father again, but will come to Him at any moment knowing that I am in the heart of God. O child, thou shalt not fear God any more when the Holy Spirit has shown Jesus in Him. (2.) That ye are in Me. That is your standing. Your nature may be frail and fickle, your sins may sometimes overwhelm, but you shall know that I am in the Father, and ye in Me, accepted in the Beloved.

> So near, so very near to God,
> I cannot nearer be,
> For in the person of His Son
> I am as near as He.

(3.) I in you." That is what I spoke of in a preceding address, the revelation of the indwelling Christ.

It is a beautiful thing to know that the 14th chapter of John begins with our mansion or abiding-place (R. V. Marg.) with God and ends with God's mansion or abiding-place with us; for the same word which is used of the mansions of the Father's house in the second verse, is used in the twenty-third verse of God's mansion in the spirit of the believer.

Men say to me, "Is not this mysticism that you teach?"

I answer, "Every mystic is not a Christian, but every Christian is bound to be a mystic, because mysticism is the indwelling of God."

Religion among the Hindus is the indwelling of God, but it disappoints them; they cannot reach it because they seek it by endeavoring for the absorption of themselves, the loss of their individuality, in God. We as Christians seek also to know the indwelling of God, but it is not by the loss of our individuality, but by the reception of God's nature as the determining power working through the individuality which He has given to us. "Ye shall know that I am in the Father, and ye in me, and I in you."

Now turn to John 16:23: "And *in that day* ye shall ask me nothing." The Greek word is: "Ye shall ask me no questions."

Up to that time the disciples kept asking questions sugested by the intellect, curious questions; but when the day of Pentecost came they did not need to ask questions with the intellect, because they saw truth with the heart.

If I am blind, I ask my friend concerning the landscape: "Are there mountains?" "Yes." "Rivers?" "Yes." "Cornfields?" "Yes." I ask question after question, and get what help I can. But when my eyes are opened, or when the light of the morning breaks, I ask no more questions about the contour, the configuration of the landscape, because I see it for myself.

Before you have the power of the Holy Ghost you will be curious about many questions; but when the Holy Ghost shall come you shall know all things clearly with the heart. I often think that woman's nature enables me to understand how we know in the power of the Holy Ghost. A man is said to reason his way, a woman by the quick glance of her intuition sees what she cannot reason, and she jumps to a conclusion to which her husband reasons his way ten minutes later. So is it with the heart when it is illumined by the Holy Spirit. The pure heart of the believer leaps to conclusions which eye hath not seen, nor ear heard, nor the reason of man conceived. The faculty of knowledge is altered: we no longer seek it by the intellect, but by the heart. The busy intellectual disputant becomes the deep intuitioner.

And then, thirdly, turn to John 16:26; *"In that day* ye shall ask in my name."

Now in the Bible "name" stands for "nature," and you are always perfectly justified in substituting the word "nature" for "name." So Christ says that when the day of Pentecost has come, we shall ask in His nature, or rather, that His nature will ask through us; and whenever the nature of Jesus asks anything of the Father, it asks that which the Father is bound to give, because He and Jesus are one.

In one's earlier life one asks for a great many things which God never gives; and we are sometimes startled, and begin to think that prayer is inoperative. But further on in life we allow our prayers to pass the test of the nature of Christ; and as one request after another arises in our hearts, we bring it into the light of the nature of Jesus, and there are a great many things that we therefore reject. I cannot ask this, I dare not ask that, I feel that they would be incongruous with the nature of my Lord, which now has become my nature, and so would ask only in the nature of Christ.

I find in my own life that I do not pray quite so long as I used. I pray more slowly. I sit, or stand or wait before God until I tell what Christ is wanting at that moment, and when in my heart, by the Holy Spirit, the prayer of my Lord is made clear to me, I take it up. I launch my little canoe upon the current of my Saviour's intercession, and I have what I ask.

There are indeed two Advocates, two Paracletes. There is the Paraclete in the heart of God—Jesus, and there is the Paraclete in the heart of the believer—the Holy Ghost; and these two Paracletes are one. When the Holy Spirit breathes your prayer, He will inspire that which it is on the heart of Jesus to entreat, and you have the perfect circle of prayer—the Father, the Son, the Holy Ghost in you, your voice raised in unison with the music of the Holy Trinity; and so the desire which emanated from God the Father, and was reflected in His nature by Christ the Son, and was communicated to you by the Holy Spirit, is flashed back from you, and you know you have the petitions that you desire of Him. That seems to me to be

THE PHILOSOPHY OF PRAYER.

But there is a fourth work of the Spirit of God. In John 15:26, 27, it is said, "He [that is, the Spirit] shall *bear witness of Me,* and ye shall bear witness."

Now the Church is in the world not to argue, not to defend God, not to stand forth as an advocate for God, but simply to witness to the truth of the unseen and eternal. And directly, brother ministers, you and I step away from that position, and become advocates pleading instead of witnesses bearing testimony, we step away from the position of power. You and I and the Church are called to bear witness to the death of Christ, His resurrection, His ascension, and the advent of the Holy Ghost. You can talk as you like about His social work, about His teaching, about the philosophy of the administration of His kingdom; but your *prime* work is to stand up before men, and say:

"I have known and tasted and handled of the death, resurrection, ascension and return of Jesus Christ our Lord."

And while you do that the Holy Spirit says "Amen."

The other day I came on a saw pit. I could see a man sawing a great beam of timber with the long saw which rose and fell, and though I could not see his confederate, I knew that down in the pit there was another man who had hold of the saw; and I could tell the rhythm and the motion of the body of the man I could not see, by noticing the rhythm and the motion of the body of the man I could see. And I saw at once that that was an illustration of the co-witness of the Holy Ghost.

When a man stands up in his pulpit and says; "Jesus died," the Holy Ghost says: "He did, and it was by Me that He offered Himself to God." When the minister says: "He rose," the Holy Ghost says: "He did: and it was by My power that He was raised and declared to be the Son of God." When we say: "He went back to God and liveth and reigneth with the Father," the Holy Ghost, brooding in the Church, says: "Yea, Amen, I have just left Him; I am in loving fellowship with Him; I and the Son and the Father are one."

O brother ministers, ever since I learned this, my work has been quite altered, because now when I enter my pulpit I go as only a very small part of the great machinery which is in operation. I have to speak, but the Holy Ghost is all the time working with me, and hence the salvation of my people does not stand in the wisdom of men, but in the power and demonstration of the Holy Ghost. If they received simply upon my putting of it, the effect would be evanescent, but when the Holy Spirit demonstrates a thing to the conscience it is permanent.

You and I were once at school. We had a problem in geometry. We might have seen at a glance that such and such a thing must be so, but we were called upon to demonstrate it, and the demonstration would be our conclusion. So the Holy Ghost establishes the word of the child, the servant of God, in the Bible class, in the mission, and in the church.

In London, in the winter, after the services of the church are over, we have our magic-lantern service from nine to ten o'clock for people whose clothes are too shabby to come among the more respectable audiences. It is so dark that Nicodemus does not mind coming in. I carefully prepare my sermon, and keep one proof of it, and give the other to my secretary, who operates from the gallery. I begin to preach. When I say: "God so loved the world that He gave His only begotten Son," I know that as I utter the words he flashes on the screen behind me a picture of the world, a globe with a scroll around it: "God is love." When I say: "Now is the time to accept this Christ," the word "now" will appear behind me. And if I speak of the Saviour's dying love and pity, instantly I know, by previous agreement, that Doré's picture of the crucified Christ is appealing to the people. I do not need to look to see if it is there, because the awe, the reverence, the silence of the people indicate to me that that great sight is represented on the canvas. My secretary demonstrates to the eye what I say to the ear.

My meaning, I trust, is distinct. You and I may go to work for God, may go into

PARTNERSHIP WITH THE HOLY SPIRIT.

The word "communion," which the minister invokes upon the people as they leave, means fellowship, common action; and the minister stands before the people in the communion of the Holy Ghost, and the Holy Ghost demonstrates the word he feebly speaks.

O men of God, mind that you are always so filled with the Spirit that wherever you go the Holy Spirit may be prepared to go with you. You know the old Welsh story of the crowded congregation that waited for John Ellis. They sent for him. The man came back to say: "I heard him talking to somebody, and I did not like to disturb him." They said: "Go again and rap." He went, and came back and said: "I heard him talking still, and I heard him say, 'I will not go unless You come along too.' " John Ellis came in five minutes later, and the One he had been talking to came with him, though no one saw Him; and they had a meeting of wonderful power. Brother ministers, never go unless He comes too.

In Acts 11:15, Peter, speaking about Cornelius and the descent of the Holy Ghost in Cornelius' house, says rather ruefully, as if he looked back on a sermon which was only half delivered:

"As I began to speak, the Holy Ghost fell."

Peter had only got through his introduction—he had not got as far as his first head—and the Holy Ghost came down, and said:

"Man, you have made a good start, and into your introduction you have put the life and death and work of Jesus. That is text enough for Me. Now stand aside, and I will finish the sermon."

"As I began to speak!" Why, I am thankful to God if I have been able to speak for half an hour, and towards the end of my sermon I can see the Holy Spirit has fallen upon my people. But oh, that we might be so filled with the Spirit and care so much about the co-operation of the Spirit that it might be with us as with Finney or Peter! It is said of Finney, more than once in his autobiography, that if he came into a large factory, or into a church crowded with people, there was such an indescribable power about his very aspect that in many cases a revival broke out before Finney could speak a word. Men, brother ministers, let us aim for that!

Now, finally, here are the seven conditions on which you may have this mighty co-operating power.

SEVEN CONDITIONS

1. You must be *Holy Ghost filled*. Peter was filled thrice; once in the second chapter of Acts, and twice in the fourth chapter. He was a Holy Ghost filled man in character, and therefore he could count on the co-operation of the Spirit.

2. You must be *emptied*. Peter was empty. He spent many days in a tanner's house. I can hardly imagine how he got into such an emptying place. In the first place, it was a very insalubrious spot. Of all hotels it is about the last place I would select. The odor would be anything but savory. And then, in the next place, as a Jew it must have been defiling to him to be in such close association with carcasses. And yet he spent many days as in a city alley; this apostle, this man who had preached through large regions, who had raised Eneas and Dorcas, got down to the tanner's house. And a man will have to come to an end of himself before the Holy Ghost will work with him.

3. You must be *a man of prayer*. Peter was a man of *prayer*. Acts 10:9: "Peter went up upon the housetop to pray, about the sixth hour." Some may think that when I say: "Do not pray so much, but take," I mean that they are to give up their lonely hours of fellowship with God. Not at all. No true experience can ever exist apart from communion with God. But mind, instead of asking for so many things that God cannot give, you will ask for a few things definitely, you will be led out in prayer, you will feel you cannot help praying for those few things, and you will have so much to do in praising and thanking God for giving you your heart's desire that

your prayer-times will tend to be longer rather than shorter.

4. You must be *willing to give up prejudice*. When Peter was first commanded to kill and eat of the creatures let down from heaven in the sheet, he said: "Not so, Lord: for I have never eaten anything that is common or unclean." But after thinking about the vision, he was willing to give up lifelong prejudices.

I have met men in my life who have refused to receive these teachings about the Holy Ghost, which in these latter days God has made known to His church. They have said with Peter, "Not so, Lord. I believe in the good old way of putting things, and I refuse to accept any further light that may break from Thy Word."

That very often stereotypes a man's power. He cannot advance with God. If Peter had refused to advance with God, God would have gone on without him. Be sure to advance with God.

5. You must be *Spirit-guided*. This also was true of Peter. The Spirit said: "Three men seek thee; go with them."

Now listen. Never take an impulse in your heart as being final. It may be of the devil, or it may be of the Spirit of God. The devil often comes as an angel of light, but you may always know when the impulse is of God, first, by its becoming a settled purpose. You may always know the devil because he asks questions. The devil always deals with notes of interrogation, and whenever you have a lot of notes of interrogation flitting about your mind, you know it is the dust raised by the devil. When God deals with you He is always definite, and the impression grows stronger every time you pray. But any impression from God's Spirit is always corroborated by two things: by the Word, and by circumstances. The Spirit of God and the Word of God are parallel lines. And if you are truly called of God, circumstances will coincide with the spiritual impulse. The inward impulse, the Word of God, and the outward circumstances will be in line. So it was with Peter. The Spirit said, "Three men seek thee," and suddenly he heard three men rapping downstairs. Always wait for the knock of the man, as well as the impulse from the Holy Ghost, agreeing with the Word of God.

6. You must be *humble*. When this Roman officer fell before Peter the fisherman, Peter lifted him up, and said, "Stand on your feet; I also am a man." There was nothing of the priest about Peter. In our country the priest is rather glad to have a man at his feet; but Peter, a sincere transparent servant of God, did not look down, but said, "Man, stand up!"

A truly humble soul is necessary for the co-operation of the Holy Ghost.

7. You must *seek the glory of Christ*.

My secretary and I agree upon our sermon for the magic lantern service before we start; and if you want the Holy Ghost to help you in your preaching, you and the Holy Ghost must agree together what you are going to preach about. If you are going to talk about social reform, I should not be at all surprised if the Holy Ghost should say, "If you are going to preach that, you must do it yourself, for I will have nothing to do with it."

You will say, "I want to preach on the last political crisis."

The Holy Ghost will answer, "Very well, go on; but

you must go your own way. I cannot help you with that."

Or you will come to the Holy Spirit, and say, "Blessed Spirit, what shall I preach from?" and there will steal into your heart the name "JESUS!" and the Holy Ghost will say, "You may begin where you like, you may deal with any historical subject you like, but you must end with the Lord Jesus Christ."

Some time ago one of my friends went out with a little boy who was leading him across the common from the railroad station to the house. My friend said to him, "Go to Sunday-school?"

"Yes."

"What did your teacher talk about last Sunday afternoon?"

"Oh, he was talking about Jacob."

"And what did he take the Sunday before that?"

"Oh, he was talking about prayer."

"Well, did your teacher talk about Jesus?"

"Oh, no," said the little fellow, "that's at the other end of the Book."

Now I hold that Jesus is not at the other end of the Book, but He is all through the Book, and every chapter and every verse and every incident in the Bible may somehow be made a road to Jesus.

I do not say that on week evenings a minister may not deal with public questions. No doubt the world will stand still until he tells it what to do. But I do think that while he has a desire for the discussion of those great problems, with the reporters listening, whether on week evening or on Sunday, for the most part—I am not offering to lay down any absolute rule, because in the case of arbitration, when fear spread over our hearts that our two great sister countries might be embroiled in strife, the pulpit spoke out and saved (as I believe) the question from becoming serious on each side of the Atlantic—but for the most part there must be the constant uplifting of the Lord Jesus Christ in His glory as the Saviour of men. And as you dare to do that simply and humbly, the power of God the Holy Ghost will witness to the living Christ in your church, in the Sunday-school. It matters little enough to God what you are in intellectual power, or natural gifts and eloquence. He simply wants a nature yielded absolutely to Him, and a voice raised for Jesus, and the Holy Ghost will do everything else.

Heart-Rest

I HAVE LEFT OUT OF MY ADDRESSES a great many themes, such as justification, and adoption, and inspiration, and the second premillennial advent, all of which I steadfastly hold. I have tried to hold up to you the doctrines of the inner life, not the objective, but the subjective, side of Christianity. But in expounding the latter you must not suppose that I do not with equal tenacity hold the objective, the former.

I hardly know how to finish this series, except by speaking upon the rest of God. If I can only be the Joshua to conduct you into rest, my work will be worthily finished; for the climax of the teaching of the inner life is always the perfect rest of the heart.

The voice that breathed o'er Eden spoke of rest. In Genesis 2:3 we are told of the rest of God, and upon that day there fell no night, because the rest of God has no shadow in it, and never terminates. God has left open the door. It stands wide open, and every heart which He has made may share in it. A rest which is full of work; but like the cyclone, all the atoms of which revolve in turbulent motion around the central cavity of rest, so do all the activities of God revolve around His deepest heart which is tranquil and serene. And it is possible, if you and I learn the lesson amid anxiety and sorrow and trial and pressure of work always to carry a heart so peaceful, so still, so serene as to be like the depth of the Atlantic which is not disturbed by the turbulent winds that sweep its surface.

Now this rest of God spoken of in Genesis was not exhausted by the Sabbath, or by Canaan; for after each of these had existed for many a century God still spoke of His rest as being unoccupied. And at last in Matthew 11:28, 29, a simple peasant (so He seemed), stood up amid a number of peasants and fisher-folk and others, and said, "On this breast of Mine is a pillow for every heavy heart. My breast is broad enough, My heart is deep enough. I offer Myself to all weary ones in every clime and age as Shiloh, the rest-giver"; for Shiloh in Him had come.

One feels that here is the accent of Deity. He says, "I am meek and lowly in heart."

And yet He assumes to Himself the prerogative of giving rest to all that labor and are heavy-laden. How can you possibly account for the meeting of humility so great with pretentions so enormous in this meekest of men unless He be more than man, the Son of God incarnate? You will notice that as He stands there upon some mountain slope, with Chorazin, Bethsaida and Capernaum on the land-locked lake of Galilee at His feet, He speaks of two kinds of rest, the rest He *gives,* and the deeper rest which He shows us how to *find*. "I will give you rest," He says, and then in a softer undertone He whispers, "Take My yoke and you shall find rest."

I will not speak now about the rest He gives—rest from the guilt of sin, rest from its penalty, rest from conviction, rest from an accusing conscience, rest from the dread and the wrath of God. That rest He gave you, beloved, when you knelt years ago at the crossfoot, and from those parched lips the dying Christ, your Priest and Intercessor, gave rest unto your soul, and being justified by faith you had peace with God through our Lord Jesus Christ.

I will not speak of this, but of something deeper, because I find that there are tens of thousands of Christians who have got the first rest, but have not got the second. They could look death in the face without wavering, but they cannot look panic, disaster, bereavement, pain or trial in the face without disquiet.

"You shall *find* rest," but you must look for it. I want to show you *where* to find it, and *how;* in three ways, which are one, for they converge in one.

I.

First. *You must take His yoke.*

Now at first sight it appears ridiculous that those who labor and are heavy laden should find rest by having the imposition of a new yoke or burden, however light. He says, "My yoke is easy, My burden is light." But then, even an easy yoke with a light burden imposed on laboring and weary souls would surely not give them rest. How can it be? Ah, listen! It is not a yoke that Jesus imposes, but it is the yoke that He Himself carried, and a yoke by the very nature of it includes two. He says then—standing beneath a yoke—to you, weary soul, "Come hither and share My yoke with me, and we will pull the plow together through the long furrow of life."

I have been told that there are farms in the West so large that you may start a furrow in the morning, and pursue it all day, and only finish it at night, returning the next day. Whether that be true or not I am not here to say, but it will serve my purpose. One day when I was at Northfield, Mr. Moody took me to Mount Hermon school. He had a yoke of beautiful white oxen, and he told me that when one of these oxen was being yoked in, if the other happened to be on the far side of the farmstead it would come trotting up and stand beside the other until it was yoked in also. Jesus stands to-day with the yoke upon His shoulder, and He calls to each one, and says, "Come and share My yoke, and let us plow together the long furrow of your life. I will be a true yoke-fellow to you. The burden shall be on Me. Only keep step with Me, and you shall find rest to your soul."

AND WHAT WAS HIS YOKE?

Christ's yoke was His Father's will. "I delight to do Thy will, O God." Now it is not to my purpose to discuss here the human and the divine side of Christ's character. But to me it is as though Christ curtained off His divine attributes, as we might allow the curtain of a theatre to drop from the roof and to shut off the whole of the stage behind. Any moment the curtain could be lifted, and I suppose you would still grant that stage to be a part of the building, but it would be curtained off for a definite purpose. So for the purposes of understanding our human life in all its aspects, our Lord voluntarily emptied Himself, laid aside the use of His divine attributes, and was content to live as Elijah, or

John the Baptist, or as you and I have to live, a life of perpetual dependence upon God.

Directly a creature lives so, it has to take God's plan, and then to take God's power. Whenever God gives a plan, He gives the soul everything which is necessary for its completion. So when Moses on the mountain saw the plan of the tabernacle, every diamond and pearl and piece of gold and silver and wood and carved work and embroidery complete, painted by the rainbow upon the cloud or standing before him like a fair vision, he knew that down below among the people he could find a duplicate for everything that he had seen. So Jesus Christ was always looking at the Father's will, the Father's plan, and then seeking by faith the Father's power. That was His yoke.

It came into evidence so often. For instance, when He healed on the Sabbath day, and they accused Him, He said, "I could not help it. My Father worketh hitherto, and I could do no other than work out what My Father wrought in." He went across the lake to give His disciples a vacation. Five thousand hungry men broke in, and in their advent He saw the intrusion of His Father's plan, and adopted it. He started for the home of Jairus. A woman with a touch arrested Him, and in her slight touch He saw again His Father's will and plan, and waited to heal her. Then He moved leisurely forward, knowing that at the house of Jairus He would have sufficient power to raise his daughter. And in the garden it was His Father's will beneath which He bowed His meek soul, saying, "Not My will, but Thine!"

In the context also there is a most lovely illustration of this. He had been wrestling from the human side (so to speak) with the great problem—why God hides things from the wise and prudent, and reveals them unto babes; and He said, "Even so, Father." The Revised Version translates it: "Yea, Father," but it ought to have translated it: "Yes, Father." Christ's life was a perpetual "YES" to God. And if you want to live a life of rest you must pace the weary furrow of your life with an upturned face, saying, "Yes, yes, yes." Always yes!

A gentleman went into a deaf and dumb institution in London to inspect it, and at the close the boys and girls were gathered at the foot of the platform. He wrote on the slate, "Why did God make you deaf and dumb, and me able to hear and speak?"

A sob went through the audience. Then a little boy came down the aisle, and took the chalk and wrote the answer beneath, "Even so, Father: for so it seemed good in Thy sight."

That boy said "yes" to God.

Someone says to me, "If I always had to do with God, I would not mind. If it was disaster, shipwreck, fire, anything which I could trust to God, I hope I am Christian enough to bow to it. But what worries me, and makes me feverish and restless, is that things come to me from my fellow men. I cannot say 'yes' to those."

Ah, my friend, you must! You will never get rest if you do not. I tried that myself once, and I found that I had at last to come to this, and to make

NO DISTINCTION BETWEEN WHAT GOD APPOINTED
AND WHAT GOD PERMITTED.

His permission and His appointments are equally His will. Job thought so, for though Satan blasted his prosperity he said: "The Lord hath taken away." Joseph thought so, for he said: "It was not you that sent me down here, but God." David thought so, because he said, "God hath let Shimei curse; let him curse." Jesus thought so, because when Judas came into the garden to arrest Him He said, "The cup that My Father giveth Me to drink, shall I not drink it?" Though it had been brought to His lips by a Judas, it had been mixed by His Father.

Now it seems to me as if you and I are enclosed in God. An arrow comes from the enemy's bow. A man that hates me writes an anonymous letter. Someone defrauds me. Some woman sets an unkind story afloat about me. The evil travels towards me. If God liked, He could let the arrow pass this way or that. But if my God opens and permits the evil to pass through His encompassing power to my heart, by the time it has passed through God to me, it has become God's will for me. He permits it, and that is His will for my life. I do not say that the man will escape his just doom. God will deal with him. I am not going to worry myself about him. In early days I would have taken infinite pains to avert the evil that men wished to do me, or perhaps to repay them, or to show that the evil was perfectly unwarranted. I confess that I have ceased to worry about it. If you silence one man you will start twenty more. It is ever so much better for peace of mind to accept the will of God, to accept His permission and His appointment, to look up into His face, and say, "Even so, Father."

Someone says, "Sir, before you go on, I want you to answer this question. Five months ago I had the loveliest little baby boy that ever mother fondled. My husband and I perfectly doted upon that little fellow. He took sickly and we hung over him and prayed for him, and did everything we could for him. He closed his eyes one day in death, and I have never been able to feel resigned since then. Am I very wicked?"

"What do you mean by 'not feeling resigned'?"

"Well, I shed floods of tears when I am alone."

"My dear woman, that is all right. Jesus wept. He gave you power to weep, and tears relieve the overtired, overwrought system. Cry on till God shall wipe every tear away."

Do you say, "Sir, I do not quite mean that; I feel as though I cannot forgive God about it. I cannot feel as though I can say yes."

"No, because you are beginning in the wrong part of your nature. God asks you to *will* submission, and the *emotions* will follow suit. You cannot begin by *feeling* resigned, but you can begin by *willing* resignation. Say to Him, 'I will Thy will.' "

"But I do not feel it."

"Never mind! Say it a hundred times a day: 'I will Thy will,' and within a week you will change your note, and instead you will say, 'I choose Thy will.' By saying that a hundred times a day for a week, you will change your note again, 'I delight in Thy will.' "

We begin by willing it, we come to choose it, and we end by delighting in it. And that is

THE SECRET OF REST.

Will you take the yoke of God today? God's will comes to us (first) by His Spirit, (second) by His Word, and (thirdly) by circumstances. And I think it is in circumstances that we are most tested. It is just there that we have to meet God, and just as in some electric light the two points have to come very close together before the light shines between them, so the point of your will and the point of God's will have to touch, and then the light of acquiescence and peace flashes out.

You know of course what a corn on the foot is—the boot rubs it, and nature throws out a shield of hard skin, which we call a corn; and the tender flesh is under the corn. There have been things in my life that fretted and worried me, and I seemed to throw out a little corn, and was strong and hard and bore up like a martyr, like a hero. But I learned that that was not the sweetest way. I was running away from God's will whenever I had a chance, and evaded it. I have learned better lately—just quietly day by day to let God's will play upon my heart, not running from it, not hiding from it, but taking it. I take His yoke.

There are some people who bear the yoke because they cannot help it; there are other people who take it. Have you taken it? Take it now by your will. You have lost your dear husband or wife, or you have lost your money, or you have lost your lover. Now it is no use running away into society. I meet with many girls who have been disappointed in love, and they have gone into society, and made themselves hard, and steeled themselves against love in every way, while they have been running away from themselves, from God. You will live to come to an end at last. You will learn to look up into the face of the Crucified, and say, "Jesus, I take the yoke."

Why, you know when you are driving a young horse,

if that horse frets and kicks, it simply gets itself into a lather, but it has to go your way after all. Much better for the young horse if, instead of plunging and kicking and fretting, it would only take the collar and the bit right away.

That is what you are—a young colt; and you are foaming and fretting and working yourself into a fury.

You will never get right in that way. Come back, and quietly take what God permits, and understand that in that there is the secret of rest; and a new tranquillity will come. You will have your floods of tears, but you will say, "I take the will of God."

"Anoint your head and wash your face." I am so very fond of that verse. We go about whining, "O dear! my suffering!" And so we give people the conception that God is very hard, and everybody pities us, and it is rather comfortable to be pitied. You feel that you are somebody if you excite somebody else's pity, and in that you get your reward. But if you anoint your head, and wash your face, and put on your sweetest look, and dress your nicest, and live your sweet orderly self, hiding your pain in your heart, God who seeth in secret will reward you openly, and you shall live to see what you thought absolutely necessary to your life to be a handful of withered leaves. I thank God for my *dis*-appointments, because I see now that they were *His* appointments.

II.

There are the two other methods by which you can find rest in your soul. The one is *by faith*. "We which have *believed* do enter into rest." Hebrews 4:3.

The point there is that faith has two hands. With one

hand faith is always handing over, and with the other she is always reaching down; the up and the down life. The angels went up on the ladder carrying Jacob's worries, and they came down the ladder bringing God's help. Mind you have the two directions in your life. Send them up, and let them come down.

Do you know what it is when you are worried to kneel down and say to God: "Father, take this," and by one definite act to hand over the worry to God and leave it there? I heard a lady say that she had been in the habit of kneeling by her bedside and handing things over to God, and then jumping into her bed and by a strong pull pulling in all the things after her. Now that is not the best way. When you really *trust* God, you put a thing into His hands, and then you do not worry yourself or Him. If there is one thing that annoys me more than another, it is for a man to say to me: "Will you do this?" And I say: "Certainly," and then he keeps sending postcards or letters to me all the time to work me up. I say, "That man does not trust me."

So when I have really handed a thing over to God I leave it there, and I dare not worry for fear it would seem as if I mistrusted Him. But I keep looking up to Him— I cannot help doing that—and say, "Father, I am trusting."

Like my dog at home: he used to worry me very much to be fed at dinner, but he never got any food that way. But lately he has adopted something which always conquers me: he sits under the table, and puts one paw on my knee. He never barks, never leaps around, never worries me, but he sits under the table with that one paw on my knee, and that conquers me; I cannot resist the appeal. Although my wife says I must never do it, I keep putting little morsels under the table.

Soul, do you know what I am talking about? That is the way to live—with your hand on God's knee. Say, "My God, I am not going to worry; I am not going to fret; but there is my hand, and I wait until the time comes, and Thou shalt give me the desire of my heart."

Take His yoke, and trust Him.

III.

And then lastly, *reckon on God's faithfulness*.

I remember so well Hudson Taylor coming to my church the first time I ever met him. He stepped on the platform and opened the Bible to give an address, and said, "Friends, I will give you the motto of my life," and he turned to Mark 11:22: "Have faith in God." The margin says, "Have the faith of God," but Hudson Taylor said it meant, "Reckon on God's faith to you." He continued, "All my life has been so fickle. Sometimes I could trust, sometimes I could not, but when I could not trust then I reckoned that God would be faithful." There is a text that says, "If we believe not, yet He abideth faithful, He cannot deny Himself." And I sometimes go to God about a thing, and say, "My God, I really cannot trust Thee about this, I cannot trust Thee to pull me through this expenditure of money with my means, but I reckon on Thy faithfulness." And when you cease to think about your faith, and like Sarah, reckon Him faithful, your faith comes without your knowing it, and you are strong.

MY PARTING TEXT

This is my parting text: "God is faithful, by whom ye were called unto the fellowship of His Son Jesus Christ our Lord." I Corinthians 1:9.

Fellowship! The same Greek word occurs in Luke 5. When Jesus was in Peter's boat on the lake, and the net was breaking with the big haul of fish, then Peter beckoned to his partner. So that we might read the text thus: "God is faithful, by whom ye were called into *partnership with* His Son." Wonderful conception—that Jesus Christ came to share my guilt and sorrow, that I might be lifted into partnership with Him forever!

If a New York businessman wanted to start his son in business in London, he would call some old and confidential clerk into fellowship with his son, and send them over together. Suppose the old clerk should take one of the most expensive sites in the city of London, put his name down for an immense rent, and open a big business, a man might come to him and say, "You have launched out?"

"Yes," he says, "I was sent to do it."

"Have you any money? Are you worth much?"

"No."

"Have you no money to fall back on?"

"No."

"Then, how do you dare to enter upon this amazing expenditure?"

"Because I have been sent by the head of our house to open this place. He told me to go ahead and that he from New York would meet all the outlay. I have worked for him for thirty years, and he has never failed me yet. He is faithful, and he will stand at my back to the end."

Now, brothers, you and I and every Christian worker have been called to rest and work in Christ. Behind you is your faithful God, and He cannot fail. If you will take the yoke of Christ, if you will hand things over to Christ, and if you will count upon God at your back, I do not mind what happens—your heart will be at rest. Like the shell which, taken from the ocean, repeats the murmur that she learned in the ocean depths, so your heart will repeat the deep sweet music of the heart of God, out of which you have come.

Moody Press, a ministry of the Moody Bible Institute, is designed for education, evangelization and edification. If we may assist you in knowing more about Christ and the Christian life, please write us without obligation to:
Moody Press, c/o MLM, Chicago, Illinois 60610.

Printed in the United States of America